*for Doreen*

17

# TIME

*with thanks + very best wishes   Fiona.*

## FIONA GRAHAM

ISBN: 978-0-9575330-0-4

Font: Papyrus

Publishing consultancy: Zoesbooks www.zoesbooks.co.uk
Design: Afterhours Artwork: art@afterhours.myzen.co.uk
Printedin the UK by Berforts Information Press www.berforts.co.uk

All enquiries to Fiona Graham: fiona@lifefulvision.com
Published by Lifeful Vision

www.lifefulvision.com

It is time

To gather the fruit

That grew from the core

That Eve was forced to drop

So many stories ago


It is time

To eat the apple

That feeds us the knowledge

That Eve was obliged to deny

So many stories ago


It is time

To apply the wisdom

That will mend the world

That Eve was made to surrender

So many stories ago

# TABLE OF CONTENTS

## INTRODUCTION

A reclusive quantum physicist, a woman artist who has known for decades that there are alternatives to the way things are, and an ancient text that contains dangerous secrets…

It sounds like the stuff of fiction.

It is not.

The ancient text really does exist and it begins with a warning:

*If you so much as scan this text, it will challenge your ignorance but offer Knowledge.*

*If you read this text, it will challenge your beliefs, but offer Understanding.*

*If you study this text, it will challenge your mind, but offer Wisdom.*

*If you implement this book, it will challenge your very existence, but you will BE.*

There have b--een times when the knowledge, understanding and wisdom contained in the text counted as heresy, and the implementation of it was life threatening. For some people, the text, and this book, which is based on it, are still heretical and so a second caution has been added:

*If you believe that your god is the one true god, please do not read any further.*

*If you decide to ignore this advice, please do not complain to the researcher, the editor or the publisher. You made your decision.*

The text challenges all manner of belief systems and assumptions, including notions of gender equality. The third and final caution is:

*This book is not politically correct.*

*If you are offended, please keep reading and pay attention to how other parts of your being respond to the words on the page. It is possible that your heart, your intuition, or your body will react positively to ideas that your mind initially rejects.*

These warnings are necessary, because the text presents a radical view of how and why the universe came to be and of the role of women within it.

Based on the text, this book is an evolutionary manifesto. As the 21st century unfolds, the environmental and institutional troubles besetting the world are glaringly obvious. They will not be solved by tinkering with existing structures, because, as Albert Einstein observed, '**No problem can be solved from the same level of consciousness that created it.**' A radical shift in thinking is necessary. The relevance of the text to the world today, is that it offers a model of how to cause such a change in consciousness.

If this book stimulates thought, further research and debate, it is beginning to do its job, but it has been written to galvanise readers into actions, which have the potential to transform the world.

\*\*\*\*\*

In translating the text, the scientist (henceforth referred to as the researcher) worked from a printed, undated, leather-bound volume. The text's custodians were aware of his work. In publishing this abbreviated version, he and the artist (henceforth referred to as the editor) have taken the difficult decision not to reveal the text's whereabouts. We are well aware that we risk accusations that we have invented it. By keeping silent, we do not associate the custodians of the text with this book. They do not share all the opinions expressed in the text, let alone those added to this book.

The printed text is anonymous and was written by several different people. They are referred to in this book as the original writers. They wrote in an archaic language, in which gender is assigned to nouns. If it was the language they spoke in everyday life with their neighbours in what is now the Middle East, then we may estimate that the writers lived some time between two and four thousand years ago. It is also possible that the writers chose this language as a private code. In this case, they might have lived much more recently and not necessarily in the Middle East. Their need for secrecy is reflected in the structure of the text, which is pleated together so that consecutive sentences sometimes jump from one theme to another.

Whoever the original writers were and whenever they lived, their description of the creation and formation of the universe appears to draw on an older, oral tradition. It is also possible that the writers journeyed, as shamans do, into other realms of consciousness and described their personal visions. They were definitely mystics, as their text is spiritual without being religious. The text echoes some of the Hindu and Sufi teachings, some of the Kabbalistic material and the Tao Te Ching, but comes to different conclusions.

The original writers were also acute observers of human nature and their comments are often wry. Both the researcher and the editor have tremendous respect for them, and have tried to do their work justice, even though this book is simplified and shortened. The researcher's translation runs to over 250,000 words, as he included all the repetitions and reiterations in the text, and added more examples from current studies that were unavailable to the original writers.

The editor has reduced the researcher's bulky tome to this short book. She has used broad brushstrokes. Since no reader is likely to be entirely comfortable with the

11

generalisations about women and men, it is important to say here that individuality is stressed time and again throughout the text. Everyone occupies a unique niche on the continuum between female and male, and has a blend of feminine and masculine qualities. These qualities were, of course, first defined by male priests and philosophers.

This book follows the original text, by omitting the animus and anima figures in the female and male psyches. The concepts of the animus and anima were introduced by the Swiss psychiatrist Carl Jung (1875-1961), who noted in his autobiography that he had never trusted a woman. In later life, Jung also admitted that he was afraid of women because they were so powerful.

*****

Part One of this book outlines the main themes of the text, beginning with the origins of the universe. Even in abbreviated form, they are mind-bending. The reasons why the original writers were concerned with the state of the world are different to ours, but their analysis of why civilization is unbalanced and how to realign it holds good today. Their remedies are simple, non-violent and radical.

Part Two opens with a summary of the essentials points made in the first part. It continues with evidence from biology, anthropology, history and sociology to support the contention that the natural roles of men and women have been inverted. It examines different religions, mentioning the changing roles of women within each of them. It then comments on the original writers' guide to transforming the relationship between women and men.

As the researcher and the editor are implementing the style of relationship advocated by the original writers, this book concludes with their personal stories.

# GLOSSARY

Each of the following terms is described in greater detail where they occur in the book. Two of the terms have been invented by the researcher, and others are assigned particular meanings within the context of this book.

____/N-One-ness – the void and source from which all things come and to which all things return

Spiritual – the essence of energy in all its forms

Matrix (plural: Matrices) – literally translated as *mother line*, the term Matrix is both abstract and substantial. It is female in nature. Like the uterus enveloping a foetus in the original mother line, the Matrix is a closed structure with something ordered inside, and is as such self-organizing.

____/Rectification – the process through which the Matrix reunites with the ____/N-One-ness at the end of its life cycle.

14

"I am" – the conscious part of the Mind, the carrier of self-consciousness and self-awareness.

"Non I" – the sub-conscious part of the Mind.

Mind – the combination of the "I am" and "non I".

# PART ONE

## THE -N-ONE-NESS

Trying to comprehend the _____/N-One-ness is not easy, especially in words, which are imprecise and limited. The "non I" is as useful a guide as the "I am," because the _____/N-One-ness goes beyond the limits of human logic and rationality. The black line which precedes the word *N-One-ness* throughout this book is there as a reminder that the _____/N-One-ness is an intangible abstract. The blank space counters the human tendency to turn an abstract into something tangible.

The _____/N-One-ness is the source of our universe and its eventual destination; it may be helpful to use two analogies that illustrate the human relationship to describe it.

1. What if a raindrop could be aware of itself separating from a cloud and falling to the earth? Would it forget that it had come from the ocean and been transformed first into vapour and then back into liquid? Would it expect to remain an individual drop after it hits the ground? Would it

resent the fact that it will eventually be reabsorbed into the ocean where it began?

2. Imagine, if you will, that you can find a way to remain yourself and at the same time call into existence other selves, which are based on you and are spiritually part of you. For the time they exist, these versions of you are independent of you and are as different to you as other people are. Their independence enables you to experience yourself from the outside, so that you gain the kind of information about yourself that you cannot gain by looking into a mirror or from listening to other people. Once you merge with all your different selves again, your understanding of yourself will be greatly enhanced.

But while the versions of yourself have their independent existence, their view of you is very different to your view of them. In order to be independent, they have developed self-awareness and self-consciousness. They could argue that they are individuals in their own right and that they wish to stay that way. They could refuse to merge with you again, as they do not want to give themselves up for your gain.

Worse, these selves could argue that you are their creator and that you created them for their gain, not yours. From their point of view, which is the only valid point of view as far as they are concerned, your purpose in creating them was that they were created. Now they expect to remain independent individuals forever, because you, their creator, will provide them with life everlasting, simply because, again in their opinion, the only reason you had for creating them was that they should be created.

\*\*\*\*\*

The _____/N-One-ness is impersonal and abstract.

The _____/N-One-ness is unlimited, undefined, infinite, outside time, outside space. Yet it IS, like a story *is*, though it is not to be found in the actual paper and ink of the book that contains it or inside the brain matter of its narrator.

The _____/N-One-ness is not nothing. It is less than emptiness and less than a void, yet it is more than both. It is the source of, but not subject to, space and time. Without the _____/N-One-ness there would be nothing whatsoever.

The _____/N-One-ness IS in the past, it IS in the future. It IS right now.

The _____/N-One-ness is not an individual and does not have self-awareness, self-consciousness, or self-worth. It does not have any survival instincts because it simply IS. It IS absolute, outside all beginnings and ends.

It is something as well as nothing yet *being something* and the *awareness of being something* are not the same. It is complete already, but lacks the capacity to know that it is complete.

If the _____/N-One-ness can be said to have a purpose, **its purpose is to become aware of itself. Human beings are a means to its end, not the end in themselves.**

In order to fulfil its purpose, the _____/N-One-ness needs something that is both 100% part of itself and simultaneously separate. This something needs to be able to return its experience of separation to the wholeness of the _____/N-One-ness.

Only by splitting itself can the _____/N-One-ness allow the something to separate. The something is called a

Matrix. The purpose of a Matrix is to develop self-conscious, self-aware, separate individuals capable of understanding themselves, their origin and their destiny. These individuals need to experience their separation fully so that they can come to understand that they are not, and never have been, separate from the Matrix.

For the ____/N-One-ness to gain awareness of itself, the knowledge, understanding and wisdom accrued by the individuals in the Matrix needs to be returned to it through a process called ____/Rectification.

The ____/N-One-ness does not think or plan how to split. As it is outside time, there is no chronological order. Instead, there is a sequence through which the potential for a Matrix begins as an impulse, a thought, which strengthens to become an idea. When the idea becomes desire, it is powerful enough to cause the potential to manifest.

Then the unchangeable ____/N-One-ness splits. In one massive burst of energy, its unity is shattered.

That which IS/was something and nothing, IS/is now something and nothing plus the something that is a Matrix.

It IS/is no longer a unity. It IS/is no longer complete and may only become complete when a Matrix finishes its life cycle and returns to the unity that the ____/N-One-ness IS and which it cannot be while a Matrix also exists.

Note that the ____/N-One-ness does not create a Matrix. Despite the human temptation to see it as the creator, it is not. It is not a god. It is not the God. It does not have the self-awareness to create. It is not malicious, unsympathetic, or cruel. It simply does not care about what it has caused to exist. Causing something to exist is very different to creating it intentionally.

The life cycle of a Matrix is determined by the amount of energy released when it split from the____/N-One-ness. When that energy has been used up, a Matrix returns to the ____/N-One-ness.

During the life cycle of a Matrix, the energy flows in one direction, through whatever processes and forms are required to develop separate individuals. The energy also provides individuals with opportunities to discover that they have always been part of the unity of their Matrix and the ____/N-One-ness. Within the Matrix's limits, the flow is flexible and moves faster or slower to allow for evolutionary developments. This "fixed flexibility flux", also called the "probability maxim of Matrices", means that there is a realistic chance, or probability, that everything possible in the set-up of a Matrix will manifest during its life cycle. In other words, if it is possible, it is more than likely to happen.

That the individuals are self-aware and separate is essential to the purposes of the _____/N-One-ness and, therefore, of the Matrix that allows them to develop. But their self-awareness and separateness cause problems.

Separate individuals think they are independent. Independence means that they cannot be controlled and it makes them selfish. Selfish individuals want to survive at all costs, and they put themselves first and last, before they think of anyone or anything else. They may or may not discover that their separation is, and always has been, illusory.

To achieve _____/Rectification, the individuals who exist in a Matrix need to learn that they are not, and never have been, separate, so that their accumulated wisdom can be returned to the _____/N-One-ness at the Matrix's end.

Then the _____/N-One-ness becomes aware of itself and of the unity that it IS and has always been.

If the energy of their Matrix is used up before the self-aware separate individuals have realized that they are and always have been part of the unity, they are reabsorbed into the _____/N-One-ness as though they and their Matrix had never existed.

Again and again, the text stresses that there is always a third option. So there is with _____/Rectification. It has not happened yet, but the prospect is appalling. If a Matrix ends when its energy is distorted and damaged by the accumulated experience of individuals' separation, it will not be compatible with the _____/N-One-ness. The unity will never mend. The Matrix and its inhabitants will be static and stuck partly before the return, partly after it, neither here nor there, in a voided non-void. The consciousness will be locked in a state of perpetual torment.

OUR MATRIX: FRAME AND FLOW

This is how the shattering of the unity that caused our Matrix is described in the original text. As the writers tried to verbalize the indescribable, they used the most paradoxical language to be found anywhere in their text.

"From the ____/N-One-ness a brilliant spark of impenetrable darkness ignited, flashing. Unfathomable, deep within the darkness of this spark, gushed a flow without substance or colour, its shapelessness forming, yet not forming, in the indefinable infinity of the ____/N-One-ness. Being, yet not existing, until the flow contracted, then emanated, into a singular Matrix and started to radiate, creating colours, and substance. Forming - developing into a finite world and calling it 'Home'."

The shattering of the unity was expressed also in a parable that tells of the separation of the upper and lower waters. The upper water stands for that which is yet to form, while the lower water represents that which is formed. The separation is not seen as a cause for celebration because, despite the necessity for the division, it divided the unity.

The split from the _____/N-One-ness released all the spiritual energy required by our Matrix in a single surge, a maelstrom that spun clockwise and counter-clockwise simultaneously through dimensions, which were not yet physical or spatial. This was the Emanation of our Matrix. It might or might not be the first Matrix to emanate. Perhaps previous Matrices failed to achieve _____/Rectification.

The single energy pulse moved and continues to move through our Matrix in a one-directional flow. At the end of our Matrix's life cycle it will return through the maelstrom to the _____/N-One-ness.

The flow of the energy through our Matrix, from its beginning to its end, is time. Although time can be measured in set units (seconds, hours, years, etc.) it has never had, and does not have, a fixed or constant speed. The fact that time flows is fixed, but *how* it flows is flexible. Thus it can be said that the fixed flexibility flux of our Matrix is the driving force behind all developments.

The purpose of our Matrix is to evolve separate, self-conscious, self-aware individuals capable of interacting with each other, in order for them to experience their separateness and to rediscover their oneness with the whole. Our Matrix set in motion the processes of evolution but it does not control how they happen.

Evolution has taken time and has gone through several phases. The next phase after Emanation was Creation. Here the energy divided, although it is important to remember that it remains essentially one despite the number of times it divides and sub-divides. All the apparently different forms it takes are interconnected.

Some of the general spiritual energy became the structure of the Matrix's other levels - Formation and the World of Interactions. The general spiritual energy can be described as one long string with many branches. Even the tiniest branch is always connected to all the rest of it and to the _____/N-One-ness.

The rest of the energy divided again and again at the Creation level to form individual spiritual energy packets. No two individual energy packets were, or will ever be, identical. Each packet became, or will become, an "I am," different to all others. Even identical twins are different at the "I am" level. Each "I am" forgets that it is connected to the whole, because its purpose is to experience separation and to have the opportunity to rediscover its connectedness.

At the Formation level, each individual energy packet adds a part of the general spiritual energy as a "non I" to the self-aware, self-conscious "I am." Together the two parts make an individual Mind.

The next level of our Matrix is the World of Interactions, otherwise known as the universe. Kept in motion by the one-directional flow of time, the World of Interactions is not, and cannot be, static. It is constantly changing and evolving.

Only in the World of Interactions can the general spiritual energy become sufficiently dense to acquire the dimensions of length, width and depth, which it lacks at all other levels of our Matrix, and to form the physical matter of our universe. The varying densities of physical matter mean that the general spiritual energy can have an enormous variety of forms.

The physical fabric of the universe provides the framework in which the Minds created during the Formation phase experience their individuality and separation. Here they also have the opportunity to gain understanding of the unity of the whole.

Our Matrix does not have any care or concern about any of the individuals that have lived and still live in the World of Interactions. Collectively and individually all of them are merely a means to an end, which is for the _____/N-One-ness to become aware of itself.

The degree to which each Mind is conscious of its existence, and of its individuality, during its life in the World of Interactions, depends on the size of the "I am" component in its individual energy package. At some point, its Mind must separate from the physical body that houses it in the World of Interactions. The physical matter is recycled according to physical laws, while the Mind, changed by its experiences of interacting with other Minds, returns to the Formation level.

The accumulated experience of Minds in the World of Interactions is held as information in the collective "non I", until such time as our Matrix returns to the _____/N-One-ness at the end of its cycle.

At the end, all the energy released in the initial burst of Emanation will reverse through the stages of Formation and Creation. What was divided into individual and general spiritual energy will reunite and go back to the _____/N-One-ness as one huge burst through the maelstrom of transformation.

To make it back through the maelstrom, the energy has to be unified as it was in the beginning, but it has been changed by the experiences that each and every individual Mind has had in the World of Interactions. This is why there are three possibilities: successful _____/Rectification, return without _____/Rectification and the failure of partial return.

# INTERLUDE

The original text repeats time and again that despite the multiplicity of more or less dense forms to be found in the universe, the energy of which they are composed is essentially one. Therefore **everything is connected**.

If this concept is new to you and you take nothing else from this book, take this: **you are and always have been part of the unity**.

You are a unique individual and so your personality, character, actions and experiences are special to you. But however separate you believe yourself to be, however alone you feel, **it is only your opinion**.

A sycamore tree stands in a field. How you see it depends on your viewpoint. You can choose to see the tree isolated in the landscape, or as a self-contained system that processes the elements required to sustain its life and to make its successors. You can see the sycamore as part of the whole landscape interacting with fungi, insects, birds and grazing animals; you can see it as energy interacting with many other forms of energy. Once you accept that you are part of the substance of the earth, part of the substance of the universe, part of the vast indefinable ____/N-One-ness, your outlook is different, your behaviour is different and your experience is different.

## EARTH AND ITS PEOPLES

This planet is only a tiny part of the World of Interactions. The first spark of life originated in the initial surge of energy that split the ____/N-One-ness and arrived here from elsewhere in our Matrix.

Earth's inhabitants may have developed into the only sentient beings in the universe. Although humans tend to believe this, in all probability there are other Minds in other parts of the universe. If any of them have visited Earth, they could be the entities, with less dense forms than humans, which have been variously called aliens, angels, demons, djinns and even gods. Humans may perhaps share this planet with forms of consciousness that have developed elsewhere in the World of Interactions.

To be born on Earth, Minds created at the Formation level come into physical bodies, which are perfect vehicles for housing and carrying them and for separating one Mind from another. Bodies have evolved, are evolving, and will continue to evolve, for the sole purpose of physically carrying and housing Minds. As bodies are vehicles for Minds, brains function as the interface between the Mind and body. Minds cannot be contained in bodies, because they have no spatial or physical dimensions and their awareness extends beyond the physical material.

A creature's level of self-awareness and self-consciousness, is determined by the portion of individual spiritual energy in its packet. The human "I am" – the conscious rational part of the Mind – has the largest portion of individual spiritual energy and therefore the strongest sense of separation, of any earthly creature. In line with the Matrix's purpose to allow for the development of separate, self-aware, self-conscious individuals, every human "I am" forgets that is part of the whole, and it may or may not relearn the connection. On the plus side, its forgetfulness prevents the overflow of information from the general spiritual energy or collective consciousness, and protects the "I am" from the madness that too much information can cause. On the minus side, the "I am's" forgetfulness keeps the individual so isolated from others that genuine empathy is difficult. Collectively, the inability of most humans to empathize with others means that we fail to learn from history and tend to repeat the same stupid blunders.

The individual "non I", or subconscious, never forgets that connection. Formed by the fusion of the body's general spiritual energy and the "non I" from the individual energy packet, an individual's subconscious absorbs without judgement all the individual's experiences. It can block traumatic memories from the conscious mind, with which it communicates through intuitions, images and dreams.

An individual's "non I" connects with the collective "non I", or general spiritual energy. This connection explains human group behaviours which resemble those of flocks of birds and shoals of fish. Through the general spiritual energy, the individual "non I" also connects with the unity of the Matrix and the _____ /N-One-ness. The collective "non I" contains the accumulated experience of everything that has ever existed. Everything means precisely that: past, present and future. Everything in the past and present can be accessed and possible futures, such as the emergence of a hybrid between humans and machines, can be anticipated.

So far, the texts have outlined a process that describes how and why humans came to be on the earth. The process has a beginning and will have an end that is not yet determined. Comprised of the same essential energy in a myriad of forms, the process causes, but does not create. There is therefore no creator god. There cannot be one.

The comfort offered by a supreme being who created this world in its image is absent, but absent too are the contradictions between the perfection of a divinity and the glaring imperfections in the world it created. Gone are loving and beneficent gods and goddesses, but gone too are angry and punitive ones. Gone is the need to please the divine and to appease it through sacrifice. Gone are the religious devotions that keep the faithful too busy for genuine spiritual experiences. Gone are all forms of afterlife in which the individual continues as an individual in any material or physical way. Gone are hopes for rewards, but also fears of punishment. Gone is a divine plan that tells people exactly where they are going. Gone are fate and all other supernatural controls over human lives.

In the absence of a creator god, human life is nonetheless spiritual, because the energy of which people and the world are made is essentially spiritual. Human life does have purpose and meaning, in that the aim is to become conscious that separation from the whole is an illusion.

But for many people the experience of the world is one of unremitting suffering, and they have looked outside themselves for explanations of why they have to suffer.

Throughout the ages, priests, priestesses and prophets have offered any number of answers to the big questions about why humans live and what happens when they die. Sometimes claiming direct and exclusive communication with the divine creator, the prophets and priests and priestesses have started local cults that gradually developed into full-scale religions, which then fragmented into different sects.

Wryly, the text comments on religion. What happened to 'seeing is believing' when the gods remain invisible? Why do omnipotent gods bother to create an imperfect world? Why do omnipotent gods need to copulate with human women for their children to be born on earth?

The writers of the text were not at all amused by suffering. They accepted some suffering as part of the human condition, but the rest they viewed as manmade. They very clearly meant male-made.

The language in which they wrote is inflected and so gender is assigned to nouns. The nouns they used for the Matrix and the energy which flows through it are consistently female. The general spiritual energy divides into female and male only in the World of Interactions. The development of male bodies to carry individual Minds has advantages for our Matrix, even though it cannot control the evolutionary process and does not care about its consequences. The World of Interactions is something of a bottleneck in the Matrix, as it took quite a time to evolve to the point where it could accommodate the separate, self-aware, individuals it requires. The division into male and female increases the range of experiences available to Minds.

The issue with male energy in the World of Interactions is that the experience of males has the potential to compromise the reunification of the energy by distorting it beyond repair.

On Earth, the division of the general spiritual energy into male and female makes sexual reproduction possible. Among humans, the body defines *what* an individual is and therefore her/his personality, while the Mind defines *who* an individual is and therefore her/his identity. Male human bodies tend to larger and stronger than female ones and male psychology tends to be more combative and competitive than that of women.

Armed with greater physical strength and a more aggressive outlook, men are able to impose controls over weaker men, women and children. To back up the use of physical force, they have invoked unseen divinities, which endow them with the right to rule. Their brutality has caused the human race an enormous amount of suffering.

The text devotes many pages to accounts of wars fought by the Hittites, the Persians and the peoples of Sumer, to show that all parties in a conflict proclaim the rightness of their cause and actions while condemning those of their enemies. The original writers were wise enough to know that there are no absolutes of right and wrong, and wise enough to notice that this statement is also absolutist. They were clear that all judgements of right and wrong, good and evil derive from religions and that no two religions agree on the definitions.

Suffering is indeed part of being human. Long droughts or sudden storms, earthquakes and volcanoes, wreak destruction on homes and crops. Illnesses can be long and painful. People die and are mourned by their survivors. Distress is, and always has been, part of the human experience.

But as said earlier, some suffering, such as the suffering caused by warfare, is manmade. It causes rifts in the fabric of the Matrix. It is not the inevitable consequence of being human. It is the avoidable consequence of male attempts to control the natural world.

The text describes an image in which the parched broken earth is dark grey below a leaden grey sky. The ground is torn by a ragged black gash, a rift of terrifying depth. On the far side of the abyss, a woman in a black hooded cloak sits on a boulder. Her face is hidden, her head is bowed in grief and mourning, for she carries the pain of the female World of Interactions under enforced male rule.

All forms of male control are rooted in fear. Men are frightened, if not terrified, by the power of nature and of women. They seek mastery over everything that they cannot comprehend, rather than admitting that they do not understand.

The text offers a remedy for the unavoidable suffering and for men's fears.

When the texts describe women they often use an adjective, which means *excellent* or *superlative*. When used in comparison to men, the word means *superior*.

Women are superior to men because they are part of the female fabric of the Matrix in a way that men cannot and never will be. Female energy filled the Matrix before the male energy penetrated the World of Interactions, so men are like immigrants to a new country, never quite certain of the customs and laws. Completely at home, women connect to the fabric of the Matrix through the substance of their bodies, and the connection makes them innately powerful. Women are able to contain males as they can give birth to both boys and girls. Men are, of course, unable to give birth to children.

The remedy for suffering, that the texts propose, is that men release their desire for all forms of control and surrender to female authority.

Male surrender to female authority benefits both the individual male and the world as a whole. It brings the man a sense of belonging, because all his actions are guided by the woman to whom he has surrendered. He is no longer a foreigner adrift in a country he cannot fully comprehend. His surrender also helps to make his energy compatible with the fabric of the Matrix, so that he can no longer create rifts.

This matters because there is no way of knowing when this Matrix will run out of time - the energy released at Emanation - and therefore when _____/Rectification may occur. While humans do not know for certain that they are the most self-aware of all beings in the World of Interactions, they need to accept responsibility for fulfilling the Matrix's purpose. Unless men surrender to women, there can be no successful _____/Rectification. Throughout the text, _____/Rectification is significant, because it brings all pain and suffering to an end in the healing of the _____/N-One-ness. As part of the unity of the whole, each individual will be part of the consciousness of the _____/N-One-ness and will BE complete and whole in a way that an "I am" in the World of Interactions cannot fully appreciate.

The proper role of men was, is and always will be to serve, support and supply women, so that women can properly attend to their spiritual duty. The proper role of women is to mend the rifts already made in the fabric of the Matrix and to prevent the formation of any further rifts. The greatest service that men can offer to women is their surrender to the female authority, because it aligns them with the natural order.

For a boy the authority is primarily his mother. She may choose to delegate some of this authority to other women. Once boys have matured into men, they pass from the authority of their mothers to that of their wives.

The text sets out rules to govern the behaviour of a surrendered man. They are designed to prevent him from doing any further harm to the fabric of the Matrix, to free him from playing roles that he is unfit for, and to maximize the amount of general spiritual energy he can channel to a woman for her to use in her spiritual work.

For a man who has not been raised by an authoritative woman, the first step of surrender is to admit verbally how he has caused unnecessary pain to women and to the world in the past. He also needs to express his willingness to atone for his previous actions, through his surrender to a woman and submission to her will.

Then or at any time thereafter, the woman may test whether a man really means what he says by asking him to do something that embarrasses him. The degree of the man's reluctance to be embarrassed is a sign of his resistance to her authority.

Once she has accepted his surrender, the woman marks the man as hers by choosing a new name for him. She may require that he be circumcised. The removal of the foreskin can only be done to a male and it is therefore a sign of his commitment.

The second step for the surrendered man is to perform a ritual at least once a day. Women are spiritual by nature but men need to practise. The man's daily ritual includes the acknowledgement that he is completely submissive to the woman's will, reflection on the rules that she has set for him, and if she requires it, atonement for his past behaviour in particular and the past behaviour of his gender in general. The ritual ends with these words addressed to the woman, *"Let the actions of my body, the words of my mouth, the thoughts of my mind and the spirituality of my existence be acceptable to you now and for the rest of my life."*

The third step requires the man to implement the tasks set for him by the woman. They can be active or passive, but they need to be continuous, as a reminder to him that he is under her authority and cannot deviate from her will. The very fact that he obeys her gives a huge boost to the energy she receives from him.

The tasks govern how the surrendered man behaves towards the woman to whom he has surrendered and to all women. They mean that the words with which he finishes his daily ritual have a real effect on how he conducts himself. It is after all easy for a man to say that he respects women and intends to change his habits, but until the words are followed by actions, they are hollow.

The surrendered man gives control over his sexuality to the woman. He is monogamous though she may choose not to be. She says when, how and, indeed, if she and the man are lovers. He is sexually passive until and unless she asks him to be active. The text recommends that they are married, but only she can decide to end the marriage. She decides which other women he may touch and what sort of physical contact he may have with them. She may feminize him by having him wear female clothing, or in any other way she chooses.

The actions of his body include how the surrendered man looks at the woman. He must not look her in the eyes without her permission. The rule exists because eye contact is one of the means men have used to control women. Keeping his eyes downcast is an act of submission to female authority. Whether or not he averts his eyes from the faces of all women is up to the woman to decide.

The woman's authority over a surrendered man extends to his actions beyond the intimate and domestic spheres. His work and leisure, in fact all aspects of his life, are subject to her command. At all times the woman needs to be vigilant to maintain and extend her authority, because male dominated patterns of male and female behaviour do damage and die hard. She must not permit him to add to the suffering caused by men. Even if her decisions sometimes appear arbitrary, he has to accept them without complaint. Given that it is her right and duty as a woman to alleviate suffering, she is unlikely to make him suffer through her choices for him.

How the surrendered man speaks to the woman is a crucial part of his submission to her. He will not use words to argue, persuade, complain, undermine or contradict. He will not lie or make excuses. He will accept what she says and obey her in what she asks of him. He will make comments and suggestions only when she requests them.

With the fourth step, the woman and the surrendered man achieve symbiosis. It happens when he has sacrificed to her the one thing he possesses in the female world – himself. By this time, he has learned that when women and men disagree, the women are always right; he has discovered from experience that female rule works so well that he does all he can to help other males to accept and adjust to it too. In other words, he has overcome all his egotistical drives. He is so utterly dedicated to channelling energy to the female, that it is akin to worshipping a Goddess in the form of a living woman. She can then add the energy she receives from him to her own and use it to heal.

A woman may accept the surrender of one man, several men or no men at all. The only qualification she needs is that she is aligned to the flow of the Matrix. The role of healing rifts belongs to her and to all women, because women are not only connected but also creative. Their creativity extends beyond making new bodies out of the matter of their own bodies during pregnancy and beyond the raising of children. Women are able to change and mould and mend the material fabric of the World of Interactions.

When and only when, a woman is clear who she is, what she is and what she desires, can she consciously create. Before using the following steps, she needs to be free of male control, sure of her motives and absolutely certain that she has the right and the ability to create.

Once she has settled in a quiet meditative state, she needs to list her goals. It does not matter whether the "I am" thinks they are achievable. There are no limits when a woman is aligned to the Matrix, for she cannot make mistakes.

She needs to leave her "non I" free to find the most appropriate means to bring her aims into reality, so she will be wise not to drift into imagining the stages by which her intentions might manifest.

As the "non I" responds to emotions and does all it can to meet emotional needs, thinking about the goals is not enough. They need to be felt as emotionally as possible. After all, the Matrix emanated from the _____/N-One-ness because of the strength of its desire to know itself as unity.

The woman can repeat the exercise of listing her aims and imagining how the manifestation of her intentions feels night and morning. While her "non I" arranges how to turn her aims from imagination to reality, she is wise to listen to and act on the promptings of her intuition.

Each woman is an individual with more or less aptitude for creating in this fashion. The technique can be practised alone or with a group of other women who share the same goals.

Only that which is aligned to the flow of energy through the World of Interactions can be manifested in this fashion. Other structures may be imposed upon the Matrix as men have done and continue to do, but everything that has been imposed is doomed to fail, sooner rather than later.

The text is clear that a world envisioned and manifested by women would be a different and happier place, because females are connected to the Matrix and can align with the energy flow, in a way that males are not and cannot. The writers do not describe such a world but they stress that it is both possible and necessary in order to achieve _____ Rectification.

## PART TWO
### IN BRIEF

The original text offers a coherent if controversial explanation of why and how humans come into being. The sequence goes like this:

*The _____/N-One-ness seeks to know itself. In other words, consciousness desires to become conscious of itself.

*Consciousness divides in a process rather like the Big Bang to form a Matrix, which, like a uterus, contains all the energy and potential required to develop separate, self-aware, self-conscious beings.

*Our Matrix may or may not be the first to split from the _____/N-One-ness. It is finite. The flow of energy through the Matrix manifests as time.

*The energy released in the split, divides over and over again, until it becomes dense enough to take on spatial dimensions and to form the universe.

*Neither the ____/N-One-ness, nor the Matrix, has an investment or interest in any individual inhabitant of the universe. The process has been set in motion and as it unfolds, anything that is possible is likely to happen.

*One of the divisions manifests in the universe as masculine, although all the energy released to that point has been feminine.

*Male humans on earth cannot fully connect with the Matrix and, instead, have tried to control it.

*The damage done by men, in their attempts to control what they cannot understand, has inflicted untold suffering.

*The rifts caused by suffering jeopardise ____/Rectification, the re-absorption of the Matrix in the ____/N-One-ness, and the realization of unity.

*The Matrix may continue for a long time, or it may end abruptly in the near future. Humans need to do all they can to ensure that ____/Rectification will succeed.

*Innately superior to men, women need to lead humanity towards ____/Rectification.

*In order not to create more rifts, men need to surrender to the authority of women.

***** 

So profound was their compassion, that the original writers did not want the inhabitants of a future Matrix to undergo the distress of separation that humanity experiences. It was very important to them that this Matrix succeeds in its purpose.

We, who are alive now, are less concerned about _____/Rectification, than the scale of the problems that beset us and our planet. The suffering of people, creatures and the land itself is overwhelming and we scarcely know where to begin to heal everything.

As the 21st century unfolds, more and more people are realizing that nothing is as stable as we once thought, and that many institutions - governments, banks, corporations - no longer serve the majority of us. Some of us sense that tinkering with the system as it is, will not to prevent economic, social or environmental collapse in the next few years. Some of us know that everything is connected and are saddened by the behaviours of those who still see themselves as separate and competitive. And still we hesitate to apply the remedy that the original text suggests. Whether the motive is the achievement of ____/Rectification or the mending of a broken world, the remedy is the same.

**Power needs to pass from men, who, from a basis of fear, seek to control the world, to women, who are better able to comprehend and change it.**

This part of the book focuses almost exclusively on this planet. It adheres to the original writers' contention, that all life is part of the process of becoming conscious. It examines in greater detail, how *power over* others has become concentrated in the hands of comparatively few men, and expands on the techniques outlined in Part One, through which women can apply their innate *power from within*. Part Two continues with an explanation of a process that underlies how life functions.

## EMERGENT BEHAVIOUR

Long before computer programmers and scientists became interested in artificial intelligence, the original writers identified the form of group behaviour that is now known as *emergent behaviour* or *swarming*. It is described here at some length because it shows how everything, from our Matrix to the cells of our bodies, functions when there is a clearly defined intention or goal, but only very basic rules to govern how the aim is achieved.

Emergent behaviour is intrinsically erratic and uncontrollable, because the groups, be they particles, living cells, insects, fish, birds or people, have no leaders. Whilst the group or swarm has no hierarchy, because no one individual is more intelligent or more powerful than any other, each member of a swarm has the information necessary for the achievement of the goal. In other words, the group's intelligence is distributed among its components.

Formed in response to external stimuli, the subtle and not so subtle changes in the environment, a swarm demonstrates the ability to adapt with flexibility to reach its defined, fixed objective. Once a swarm has achieved its objective, the individuals that were part of it may disperse, or they may mill about randomly until the next objective is identified.

Careful observation of swarms, such as shoals of fish and flocks of birds, shows that they follow basic rules that are part reflexive and instinctual, and part based on experience or training. The rules start with the basics: stay close to other individuals but do not touch them. Swarming like this works well for prey species, because it confronts their predators with the hunter's dilemma – too many moving targets to choose from. Starlings flock before roosting at night, because hawks are often waiting for them to land. When the flock settles into its roost, a few individuals are caught and eaten by the hawks, but overall the individual is safer in the flock than if it returned to the roost by itself.

Additional rules apply to different species, such as ants and termites, and also within the super-swarm of the human body, which contains many sub-swarms in its organs and fluids. The nerve cells in the human brain do not change neighbours, like fish in shoals or birds in flocks, as they are fixed and linked to each other by neurons. Nevertheless, the cells swarm to create new connections, if the brain has to perform a new function or if part of it is injured.

What appears to be solid is revealed by an electron microscope to be anything but. Particles, atoms and molecules move about in constant but random motion, until they are stimulated to swarm. If, for example, you nick your finger while you are chopping vegetables, the cells around the cut swarm in order to mend it.

Humans like to think of themselves as independent individuals and value freedom of choice. We may inhabit bodies that are a collection of swarms, but we tend to see emergent behaviour as chaotic or anarchic. For individuals caught up in a mob on the rampage, it can indeed be very scary. We prefer to ignore the facts that we are connected to the whole, that we have less conscious control over our lives than we think, and that we often demonstrate swarming behaviour. Rather than accept that the leaderless, uncontrollable swarm can effectively achieve its purpose because it retains flexibility, we have developed highly organized, hierarchical social structures that are slower to respond to changes in the environment.

The way in which human swarms function, has been tested by instructing large numbers of people to walk around a large area. They were told to obey the basic rules of swarming – to stay with an arm's length of at least one other person, without touching or communicating with anyone else by word or sign. A small number of the participants were told to converge on a specific place at a certain time. When the time came, the whole group converged very quickly at the designated place, although the majority had no idea that they had been led there.

A crowd swarms to a convergence point when approximately a quarter of its members know the intended destination. When only 10% know what to do and where to go, part of the crowd converges and the rest are quick to join them once the critical mass is reached. When up to 20% of a group are told to converge at one place, and up to 10% of the remainder are told to converge elsewhere, those without instructions tend to move towards the 20%. Then, some people move towards the 10%, while others drift from the 10% to the majority. Without clear purpose, humans tend to mill about as aimlessly as the cells observed under the electron microscope.

Repetitions of these experiments showed that they only worked when women were among the participants or the observers who set it up. When no women knew what to expect, the experiment failed. The group did not converge.

The importance of female participation for the success of these experiments tends not to be mentioned in the main research papers, but it has been noted in the discussions afterwards.

People swarm at levels other than the physical. Consider how we swarm around new trends in fashion, music and culture generally, communicating via both the conscious "I am" and the subconscious "non I". The military and the marketing men are among the backers of research into emergent behaviour and the workings of the subconscious mind. Awareness of how to steer a swarm to fulfil a chosen purpose can be used for the benefit of humankind or its detriment. Knowing how emergent behaviour works and how swarms can be guided (or, depending on the motive, manipulated) is one key element to changing the world.

Emergent behaviour may also function in the creation of software. A programmer may set the goal, and then let the information that is distributed to the bytes, arrange how the programme actually runs, though the result may or may not conform to the programmer's expectations.

Like the body, our Matrix can be described as a super-swarm, because it has a purpose, but no control over how or if its intention is fulfilled. In addition, the intelligence of the Matrix is distributed through the individual and general spiritual energy.

Understanding our Matrix as an emergent process, reconciles the spirituality and the unity at the heart of most religions with much of the scientific data and speculation about our origins. It accounts for the elegance of the universe's geometric structures, and the precise combinations of elements, which allow life to flourish on this planet in such abundance and diversity. To regard the Matrix as a super-swarm will explain its lack of interest in the individuals it contains. From the single-celled amoebae, to the trilobites, to the dinosaurs to the mammals, all life forms are merely stages on the journey towards consciousness.

So here we are, unique individuals, muddling along in an evolving Matrix, simultaneously separate and yet part of a unity becoming conscious of itself. While we try to make sense of it all, we find ourselves on the brink of catastrophe, because our ancestors and we ourselves have inverted some of the basics facts about our lives and purpose.

## THE HUMAN DEFAULT SETTING

Every person is an individual, with a unique place along the spectrum of female to male, but in this short book, generalizations are inevitable in distinguishing between women and men. There never has been equality between the sexes. They are too different. They are so different that sometimes each appears to the other like a separate species. The original writers' opinion was unequivocal: women are superior to men. In more modern, but less contentious terminology, it may be said that the default setting for humankind is female.

In the human genome, XX and XY are opposite ends of a scale, with a wide range of possibilities in between. If you look as dispassionately as you can at the symbols XX and XY, what do you notice?

You may well see that a Y is an X with a leg missing. You may well accept that symbolically XX for female is stronger than XY for male.

The strength of the female goes beyond the symbols. Consider the following:

*A cell that contains only a Y chromosome has a shorter existence than a cell containing an X chromosome.

*Women tend to live longer than men.

*Women and girls tend to be healthier than men and boys.

*Men are less resilient to shock and stress than women.

*Organs transplanted from male donors to female recipients have a ten times higher probability of failure than those transplanted from females to males or from and to people of the same sex.

One strong indication that the default setting is female, lies in the mitochondrial DNA. Mitochondria are organelles (literally, *little organs*) in the structure of cells. The mitochondrial DNA is separate from, and independent of, the DNA in the nucleus of its home cell.

In human cells, the function of the mitochondria is to initiate the death of the cell and, therefore, to determine its mortality. Cell by cell, the state of the mitochondria has implications for the health and life of the whole individual.

Mothers pass mitochondrial DNA on to daughters and sons, but only daughters can pass it on to their offspring. The mitochondrial DNA has been traced back, to show that all homo sapiens alive today came from one woman, the so-called Mitochondrial Eve, who lived in Africa about 200,000 years ago. Every woman who has no children or who has only sons ends a line of mitochondrial DNA.

In human reproduction, half the DNA comes from the male and half from the female, and the female also supplies the egg cell, which contains mitochondrial DNA. Each male sperm contains about 100 mitochondria in its tail. They determine when the sperm dies. Even if the sperm is the one that fertilizes the egg, its mitochondria and their DNA are destroyed, because the egg has its own mitochondria already.

For the original writers, the possibility that women can reproduce asexually was a significant indicator of their superiority. Across the world, religions such as Hinduism,

Buddhism and Christianity, as well as cults, such as the cult of Attis, and legends, for instance those of the Ojibwa people, tell of virgin births and/or the ability of women to bear children, including sons, without intercourse with a man.

Asexual reproduction or parthenogenesis occurs naturally in plants, invertebrates and vertebrates, and it can be induced in mammals if an electrical or chemical stimulus is applied to fuse two eggs. Too much calcium in the blood can trigger the fusion of two eggs in women.

Parthenogenesis is used to create embryos for stem research cell. Since the Catholic Church issued *Donum Vitae* in 1987 and *Dignitas Personae* in 2008, stem cell research has become so controversial that if parthenogenesis in human embryos has actually occurred, it is not mentioned openly in the scientific literature.

Women may be able to reproduce asexually, but it is, of course, the ability to conceive, carry and deliver babies that most differentiates female from male and is the decisive factor in proclaiming female superiority. As noted by feminist writers, the English words *female* and *woman* are derived as adjuncts to *male* and *man* but they also contain *male* and *man*. Women are able to contain both male and female children, but every individual who has a Y chromosome, along with one or more Xs, cannot have a child naturally.

Women's bodies have the capacity to form new lives out of the matter of their own. Although pregnancy is essentially a passive process, some would say that making a baby is the most creative of all human actions.

Whether they bear children or not, the connection that women have, through their bodies, to the ground of their beings means that they are at home in the world, in which men are like immigrants.

Some, maybe many, maybe the majority of women already know that they are superior to men in some or many ways. Some men know it too.[1] However, women do not readily admit it in mixed company, because in other ways they have come to believe what men tell them.

Dependent upon their mothers for their very existence, men have an ambivalent relationship with women's bodies. They desire them, they are disgusted by them, they are in awe of them, they fear them and they cannot completely control them.

Nevertheless, men try to control women. Very often they succeed, because the Y chromosome usually provides them with larger, stronger bodies and bigger brains than women. In Europe, the average male brain is around 113 grams heavier than the average female brain, but the weight of a woman's brain tends to be a greater percentage of her total body weight.

To the original writers, male control over women was an inversion of the proper relationship between the sexes and the cause of many of the world's misfortunes.

Men's attempts to control women and the world around them are rooted in fear.

## THE FEAR FACTOR

### The World of Interactions is a very scary place.

Everything that lives kills other life forms to survive and human beings are prey as well as predators. Fear is very useful, when it helps an individual to stay alive. It keeps an

"I am" watchful for a pride of hungry lionesses, for a snake lurking in the long grass, for a car taking a corner too fast, for whatever can threaten its life.

Survival can be seen as a struggle against the forces of nature more easily than as a co-operation with them. As farmers and gardeners know, tending the land can be heart breaking as well as back breaking. The forces of nature can be so extreme and violent that the "I am" protects itself by trying to minimise its dependence on an unstable planet. Intent on its own survival, the "I am" is also loath to acknowledge its dependence on others and the importance of sharing.

The "I am" has many reasonable fears about physical survival, but it tends to add mental fears about everything it does not understand, about its future and what might or might not happen. From the body that carries it to the meaning of its existence, the "I am" can find plenty to worry about.

The "I am" regards the body that experiences as many aches and pains as pleasures, that demands to eat, expel waste, sleep and mate, that ages and will inevitably die, as frightful as well as frightening. Reluctant to identify with the body, the "I am" forgets that its body is only a more dense form of the same material or energy.

The "I am" fears change, even though change is constant and inevitable. It is reluctant to change until conditions in its present reality become intolerable. Fear of change drives all resistance to novel ideas and different ways of living.

In addition to the "I am's" existential fears, the difference between the XY and XX chromosomes leads to gender specific fears.


## MENSTRUATION & CHILDBIRTH

Men's ambivalent relationship with women's bodies begins very young, as the male children learn that they are not the same as their mothers and must separate from them. At some stage in their lives, most likely during adolescence, boys discover that women bleed during their child-bearing years.

Like the waxing and waning of the moon, women's energy levels peak and trough through their menstrual cycle.

Before biologists could explain the hormonal changes that cause the expulsion of the womb's lining, women's ability to lose blood when they were not injured appeared to men to be mysterious, almost magical.

Inside the body, blood carries oxygen and other essential nutrients and delivers waste products to the kidneys for elimination. If too much of it drains from the body, its loss leads to death. Outside the body, blood is so rich in nutrients that it quickly becomes a breeding ground for bacteria, which can spread disease. Throughout history and across cultures, blood was, and is still, seen as both powerful and polluting. Blood is so significant to humans that it has acquired an actual or symbolic role in the rituals of many religions. Blood sacrifice is intended to appease the divine and to atone for sins.

Menstruation is a manifestation of the power of the XX chromosome, connecting women to their bodies and to the fabric of the Matrix. In societies connected to the earth, the onset of menstruation was sometimes a cause for celebration as girls passed into womanhood and menarche, loss of virginity and childbirth were regarded as the natural initiations of girls and women. According to a

Native American saying: *at menarche a woman enters her power, through her menstruating years she practises it and at menopause she becomes it.*[2]

Sobonfu E. Some[3], comes from the Dagara people of West Africa, her teachings emphasize the importance of community and recognizing spirit as the life force in all living things. She describes menstruation as the time when a woman is especially capable of healing and seeing into things deeply. During menstruation, a Dagara woman is traditionally treated with respect. The man who makes love with a menstruating woman is likely to be harmed unless his spiritual energy is high enough to meet hers.

In traditional male initiation ceremonies in parts of Australasia, men cut their penises, testicles or upper thighs until they bleed.[4] Some anthropologists see this practice as an imitation of menstruation rooted in male jealousy. In many cultures, boys were formally initiated into manhood by rites that were painful and frightening to show them what women endured in childbirth.

In many societies women were either able, or obliged, to retreat into seclusion during their periods. The time apart from their normal responsibilities may be seen as either a woman's chance to rest and to contemplate, or as something that is forced upon them by men who regard them as unclean.

Other taboos have been applied to women while they are 'impure,' including abstinence from intercourse, exclusion from places of worship, bans on touching sacred objects, and cooking. Jewish women remained unclean until they had taken the ritual bath, at least seven days after their periods ended. To the Catholic Pope Gregory I (540-604 CE), menstruation was a pollution of nature, although it could not be a sin because it was natural.

The shame that women have been made to feel about menstruation, by religions, continues in the hectic world of corporate capitalism. Women bear the curse as discreetly as possible, without honouring the decrease in physical energy caused by blood loss, the natural fluctuations of their emotions and moods, or the need for quiet, private contemplation. When women are shamed into denying menstruation and menopause, they are denying their innate power.

Ignoring the wisdom of the body, causes many of the menstrual problems that women can experience. The denial of physical and emotional needs during menstruation and menopause, may lead to the kind of temperamental outbursts that upset other people and cause men to refer disparagingly to female hormones.

The shaming of women about menstruation, is only one of many ways in which men rob women's power. Another is to keep women pregnant. Pregnancy, childbirth, childrearing and domestic duties are exhausting, especially if combined with paid work outside the home.

In hunter-gatherer or foraging societies, women tend to breastfeed until their children are three or four years old. Lactation does not invariably prevent ovulation, but it does help women to space out their pregnancies. It is worth noting that hunter-gatherer groups are often egalitarian. For instance, among the peoples on the island of Luzon on the Philippines, women have been observed not only hunting and fishing alongside the men, but also carrying carcasses.

Among the many changes that occurred when humans settled in agricultural communities about 10,000 years ago, the family began to take precedence over the group. Men wanted to be certain that they were indeed the fathers of the children that lived under their roofs. They still do. To this end, they have placed all manner of restrictions on their wives and daughters that have affected women's relationships with the source of their power, their bodies.

One of the consequences of patriarchal family structures is the high birth rate that has led to the 7 billion plus humans alive on the planet. Where women are deprived of autonomy over their bodies, they have more children than in situations where they have choice. Those who think the planet is overpopulated, would do well to support the empowerment of women.

Even where women can choose to limit the size of their families, pregnancy and childbirth are often treated more like illnesses than natural processes. Beyond doubt, medical intervention does save the lives of mothers and babies, but the overemphasis on what can go wrong may cause pregnant women to have undue fears about vaginal delivery. Across the world, more and more women rich enough to pay for the surgery, are opting for C-sections, without fully appreciating the consequences. If, for instance, they are wrong about the date of conception, the baby may be removed from the womb before 39 weeks' gestation, which has life-long implications for its health.

Elective C-sections are only one example of how women have come to distrust the wisdom of their bodies. For generations, women have been told that their bodies, their hormones and their emotions make them filthy, irrational and hysterical and they have come to believe this.

Where women are not able to express their power openly, they wield it covertly, by exploiting their desirability and their roles as mothers. Men can feel manipulated, even blackmailed, while simultaneously assuming they are entitled to the sexual and domestic services of women.

Despite the strides made by feminists (female and male alike) towards equality, inside patriarchal structures the XX gene is still accorded lower status. Women who are sexual and independent, argumentative and fierce in asserting their needs, make themselves targets. They are labelled as witches, fiends, wicked and evil. They risk being assaulted verbally and physically. At worst, they risk being killed. Women who rely on the patriarchy are as critical of their wicked sisters as men are. Such women have accepted that it is their role to conform to what men tell them: women ought to be beautiful, subservient, loyal wives and good mothers.

## HISTORY & MYTHOLOGY

This section offers an unusual interpretation of history and pre-history to chart the rise of patriarchal structures and the consequent changes in the status of women. For three reasons, it draws primarily on material from Eurasia and makes few references to other parts of the globe. First, the original writers would appear to have come from that region of the world. Secondly, the area between the eastern Mediterranean and India was the birthplace of the six world religions to which, at the start of the 21st century, two-thirds of the people on earth claim allegiance. Thirdly, Europe exported not only Christianity, but also its military and economic power.

In this interpretation, no blame for what happened is attached to any individual, tribe or nation. If human development has been impelled at a very deep level to fulfil the Matrix's purpose, the subspecies 'homo corporatus', currently running the world, looks like the perfect vehicle to teach the rest of us the importance of cooperation and unity.

History was written by people who could write. In most cultures, for most of the centuries since the invention of writing around 3000 BCE, only administrators, those dedicated to the religious life, merchants and some members of the nobility were literate. The vast majority of the literate were male.

History, as feminist historians[5] have made clear, is biased towards the male view of the world. It is easy to forget that history is a matter of opinion as the 'facts' are always open to other interpretations. It is also easy to forget that history is the written record of only 5000 years and homo sapiens have been around some 200,000 years. Behaviours that appear to be normal, because the written records focus on them, are not the only behaviours possible for people.

The history we have been taught is incomplete, there is little mention of the workers who made possible the victories, discoveries and adventures in the school textbooks. Everyone who has ever lived and died a more or less dreadful death, was a unique individual whose experiences in this world contributed to the collective consciousness, and thus to the unity of the whole. The empires that have come and gone, the wars that were won and lost, all the achievements and misdeeds of the famous were built on the seasonal round of planting and harvesting, of raising stock, of mining, of making, of selling and buying – in other words, on the drudgery of forgotten men. And, of course, on the work of forgotten female drudges who bore and raised the children.

Although largely obscured, there are hints in the written and archaeological records of what the researcher calls the Original Story, a time when the relationship between women and men was other than it has become. This section and the next lift the veil on the Original Story.

Once upon a time, there might have been a golden age, when humans led nomadic or semi-nomadic lives in harmony with the earth. More probably, there was no golden age, only a different sort of struggle for survival.

Anthropological studies of the few extant hunter-gatherer tribes, suggest that women and their work are respected and that gender roles are quite fluid. Maybe women and their work were likewise honoured when small bands of people lived by foraging.

Just because a process is natural does not mean that it is gentle, so harmony with earth has to take into account the storms as well as the sunshine. Pre-historic people were as attuned to their environment as the remaining indigenous peoples of the world still are. They had to understand the environment to survive. Their spiritual practice probably revolved around respect for the forces of nature, including special rocks, water sources and the animals that they hunted and that hunted them.

The paintings in the Chauvet caves in France, which date to about 30,000 BCE, reflect the respect that people had for animals. Among the earliest known works of art, the paintings appear to have been merely the backdrop for rituals that were held in a cavern deeper into the cave system. One theory indicates that, due to the position of skulls found in the lower cavern at Chauvet, it was used to venerate bears, which, like humans, walk upright and are both predators and prey. The Circumpolar Bear Cult is one of the longest, continuous, spiritual practices that has been documented. Perhaps the last of its kind, the ritual killing of a bear, which had been raised as the village pet, was filmed in an Ainu community in the 1920s. For the Ainu people of northern Japan and southern Sakhalin, and probably for their predecessors, the bear cult was not a religion: the bears were honoured, even venerated, as lords of the forest[6] but not worshipped as gods.

The 20 structures found so far at Göbekli Tepe in Turkey have been hailed as the world's oldest religious structures. Construction of these round buildings began between 14,000 and 12,000 years ago. Four out of 20 have been excavated and they indicate that, like the Chauvet caves, Göbekli Tepe was a place for group rituals. In use for about 4,000 years, the site was deliberately backfilled before it was abandoned. Whatever the people of that area believed, their shared belief was important enough for them to come together to build, to use, and, finally to bury the site.

The role played by women or by the Great Mother Goddess in early rituals is unknown and unknowable. Certainly, many figurines depicting females, some very voluptuous, suggest that fertility and fecundity were honoured. Whether the figurines represent women or goddesses is a matter for debate. Feminist archaeologists and historians[7] argue for the power of the Great Mother Goddess, although it does not necessarily follow that, where the goddess was worshipped, women were also honoured and respected.

Skeletons found at Çatal Höyük in Turkey, indicate that women and men had equal access to food, but do not prove that society was matriarchal or matrilineal. Çatal Höyük, which probably had between 5000 and 8000 inhabitants at any one time, was occupied from about 7500 to about
5700 BCE.
The shift from foraging to farming began after the end of the last ice age, about 12,500 years ago. It is likely that average life expectancy fell when humans settled in agricultural groups, because they succumbed to diseases contracted from contact with domesticated animals, and spread by higher concentrations of people.

Settled peoples are even more dependent upon the forces of nature than nomads, who are able to move elsewhere in times of drought or flood. Nature is both bountiful and capricious. All the goddesses and gods ever invented display the same dichotomy.

A tale written on a clay tablet, found at Nineveh in Sumer, reveals the double nature of the goddess, named, in this case, as Ninhursag.

*Enki, the Lord of the Sweet Waters, lived in Dilmun, from whence flowed the four world rivers including the Tigris and the Euphrates. In Dilmun, where death, war, violence and harm were unknown, Enki loved first Ninhursag, then their daughter Ninsar, then their granddaughter Ninkurra, who also gave birth to a daughter of Enki's named Uttu. When in due course Uttu also became pregnant by Enki, she turned to Ninhursag for advice. Ninhursag suggested that Uttu wipe Enki's seed from her womb and bury it deep in the earth. But Enki's seed grew into plants and when Enki saw them they looked so appetising that he ate them. Ninhursag was so furious with him that she cursed him. Eight of his organs began to fail and he became very ill. The other gods could do nothing to ease Enki's suffering for only Ninhursag had the power to heal him. Eventually, she relented of her anger and went to Enki. She wrapped herself around his body, drawing his pain* into her. From each of his failed organs a deity grew, four goddesses and four gods. One of the goddesses was named Ninti, for she came from Enki's damaged rib. In Sumerian, her name means the lady of the rib and the lady of life, as ti means both rib and life.

From Egypt and India come two similar stories of the power of the goddess when she is enraged.

Demons or evil men terrorize the world. The gods wring their hands, powerless to bring a halt to the wickedness that they have unleashed into the world. Eventually, they realize that male energy causes damage which can only be healed by a female. Each of them channels the essence of himself into a Goddess called Sekhmet in Egypt and Kali in India.

In an orgy of killing, the Goddess fights and destroys the evil. She then goes on to kill the good too.

The Egyptian story says that the gods offered Sekhmet alcohol and that she drank herself insensible.

In the Indian story, Shiva incarnates as a baby, thereby surrendering himself utterly to Kali's immense power. His helplessness stops her killing spree.

On the subject of ancient Egypt, it is worth noting that from about 3000 BCE to about 300 CE, women enjoyed more legal rights than their sisters in Sumer, Persia, Greece or Rome. Although they were expected to marry and to be faithful wives, they owned and controlled their own property.

Around five thousand years ago, people began to live in cities, such as Uruk and Ur in Sumer. The greatest cities in the Fertile Crescent had populations of up to 200,000 people. As civilization developed over the next few thousand years, the land around the cities became the property of its rulers, priests and nobles. As property had to be defended, so military might became important. Armies needed not only leaders, but also organization and, as concentrations of civilians also had to be ordered and regulated, so bureaucracies were born. Society became more stratified and hierarchical as leaders proclaimed themselves kings, their followers became subjects, and the conquered or landless became slaves. Work became more specialized. The cities were not self-sufficient, so food and luxury goods were traded. Merchants and other travellers helped in the exchange of ideas throughout the Fertile Crescent and beyond. Men were established as the heads of their families.

And as civilization developed, the Great Mother, if indeed she ever had the pre-eminence suggested by some historians, was gradually replaced by a plethora of gods and goddesses and eventually by versions of one supreme God.

The shift from goddess to god may be associated with the development of cuneiform in Sumer around 3000 BCE. One of the earliest extant works of literature, the *Epic of Gilgamesh*, appears to offer some confirmation of this theory.[s]

Gilgamesh is regarded as one of the first solar heroes, fighting against the forces of nature, including death, and struggling to free his consciousness from the primal matter of the Great Mother. He might have ruled in Uruk around 2700 BCE. Poems about him date from about 2000 BCE and the 12 tablets that tell his story date from about 1300 BCE. By the time a Babylonian scholar called Sin-Leqi-Unnimni wrote the story on the 12 tablets, Gilgamesh was considered to be part divine and part human.

In an early story, dated to around 2000 BCE, Gilgamesh cut down a tree whose occupants – a bird, a demon and a snake – had been annoying the goddess Inanna or Ishtar. He used the wood to make a throne for her.

According to Sin-Leqi-Unnimni, Gilgamesh killed Humbaba, the spirit appointed by the gods to protect a forest, and rejected Inanna's sexual advances, because she had treated previous lovers cruelly. She turned against him and in their subsequent battles, his closest companion Enkidu was killed. Mourning his friend, Gilgamesh set off on a quest to find eternal life, but discovered that he could not even defeat sleep when he failed to stay awake for seven days and nights.

In the older story, Gilgamesh co-operated with Inanna. In Sin-Leqi-Unnimni's later story, he rejected and fought against her.

The early Sumerian myths reveal that goddesses, and probably women too, were held in 'great esteem.'[9] The decline in the status of women is charted in the different law codes that have been found.[10]

In all but the most repressive of regimes, lawmakers-kings, senates or parliaments - have to accept that only laws that can be enforced will be effective. Therefore, they have to phrase legislation in terms which are acceptable to the majority of the people, on whose support they depend.

The earliest law codes yet discovered come from the city of Lagash. They are often attributed to Urukagina who ruled the city state for about 8 years around 2380 BCE. Urukagina, who might have started life as a peasant, appears to have led a revolt against the previous king, and he bolstered his right to rule by claiming divine right from the god Ningirsu. As Lagash was under constant threat from Uruk throughout Urukagina's reign, and as he needed to please those who had supported his rise to power, he introduced a set of reforms intended to protect the weak from the strong, particularly from priests.

One tablet, on which the name of the king is illegible, may pre-date Urukagina by a few decades, as it may have been written by an earlier king called Enmetana.[11] Whichever king wrote the tablet is less significant than what it says: the custom of former times that allowed women to marry two men is to be discontinued. This line has been translated, mistakenly, as banning the taking of two wives by men. But the researcher is absolutely clear that the tablet refers to polyandry, not to polygamy, and that there is no punishment for the women.

The existence of the law implies that up to that point in time, some women in and around Lagash did have more than one husband. The original text, which may in part predate Enmetana and Urukagina, states that a woman may choose to have several men under her authority. Also, she chooses whether the men in her 'court' are her lovers, because they can serve her in a variety of ways other than the sexual. Women who held court in this fashion would have been powerful, and the men upon whom the kings of Lagash depended might well have seen these women as over-powerful. Hence the law.

Ur-Nammu, or his son Shulgi, who were kings of Ur between 2100 and 2050 BCE, formulated a set of laws. Ur-Nammu claimed his right to rule by the 'might' of the moon goddess Nanna, and the 'true word' of her son, the sun god Utu. The prologue to the law code declared the king's intention to banish wrongdoing and to protect the lowly from the strong, so that 'the widow was not delivered to the mighty man.' The laws make it clear that women were subject first to their fathers and then to their husbands. In other words, the patriarchal family was legally endorsed. In an adulterous affair, the woman faced death, but the man went unpunished. If a husband accused his wife of adultery, she faced the so-called River Ordeal. The woman who sank was guilty: the woman who floated was innocent.

Hammurabi, the sixth king of Babylon, ruled around 1750 BCE. His law code was inscribed on a huge stele, which also depicts him receiving it from the sun god, Shamash. It was displayed in public, to be read by those who could read. Hammurabi intended that justice should prevail in order to banish evil and wickedness. Although innocence was assumed until guilt was proven, the range of punishments was based on retribution – an eye for an eye. As in Ur, women were the property of their fathers and husbands.

The laws of Tiglath-Pileser I (1114-1076 BCE), king of Assyria, placed tight restrictions on the movements and contractual rights of women of high social status, who were to be veiled in public. If women of a lower class, such as maids and prostitutes, wore veils, their garments could be seized, they could be beaten and bitumen could be poured over their heads. Whereas Hammurabi's code referred to prostitutes as the sisters of a god and offered them some legal rights, Tiglath-Pileser's laws distinguished more harshly between the virtuous woman and the whore. It is a split that bedevils relationships between men and women to this day.

In Tiglath-Pileser's code abortion was proscribed. A woman who 'dropped that which was in her' faced crucifixion. A man who punched his pregnant wife and caused her to abort was fined. A man who hit a prostitute and caused her to abort had to make restitution for the life he had destroyed.

The law codes from Enmetana or Urukagina to Tiglath-Pileser show how women lost much of the authority they had once enjoyed. Somewhere in the process of civilization, the gulf between women and men deepened, matter and spirit were split, and evil entered the world.

THE HISTORY OF RELIGIONS

The writers of the original text were profoundly spiritual but not religious. Religion and spirituality are not the same. The former tends to subsume the latter, by setting spiritual experiences within a context defined by doctrine. Writing at a time when religions were a major factor in the control of the few by the many, the original writers devoted much of their text to a critique of religion.

This section updates and expands their work. It examines how the sense of oneness with the world was lost, how evil entered the world as spirit was split from matter, and how complex the roles of women within religions have become. Hinduism, Judaism, Buddhism, Christianity and Islam regulate how their adherents are supposed to behave and have legitimized male control over women.

Humans are essentially spiritual, and once the basic needs for food and shelter are met, we tend to seek explanations for experiences beyond our five senses and answers to our philosophical questions. At a fundamental level, we need our lives to have meaning and purpose, and we want reassurance that death does not equal obliteration. Religions have developed in large part to meet these needs, although each offers different, often conflicting, answers.

Both the following statements have a degree of truth. Humans invented their gods and goddesses. To the extent that they are believed in, gods and goddesses exist. In other words, all divinities are archetypes in the collective consciousness. Such power as they have, derives from the strength of their devotees' faith. With attention, a divinity grows; without it, a divinity fades. Miracles can and do happen, not because a god or a saint answers a prayer, but because the person saying the prayer has faith.

There is a theory that religious belief progressed from 'primitive' animism (the belief that everything has a spirit) and totemism (the belief that an individual or a clan has a guardian, often an animal or an ancestral spirit), to pantheism, and then to monotheism. Whether the theoretical progression is an advance in human development, or a loss of connection with the whole, is a matter of opinion.

Whilst shamanism[12] may be regarded as a survival of ancient animistic and totemic beliefs, the fact that shamanic practices continue, strongly suggests that it is natural for humans to contact levels of existence beyond the usual five senses in altered states of consciousness. The way that traditional shamans work, varies from the Arctic to the Andes, from the rainforests of Borneo to the Himalayas. Central to the practices are soul journeys, in which the shaman goes out of body in a trance, for purposes as diverse as healing, soul retrieval, negotiating with spirits for good hunting and entertainment.

Men and women can become shamans, though many resist the call as the initiations and the work are demanding and dangerous. Essential to initiation is a process of spiritual death, sometimes accompanied by the dismemberment of the spirit body, and rebirth.

Generally, shamans accept that every living thing has a spirit that exists in levels of consciousness beyond the normal concept of five-sense reality. The spirits of the dead join the ancestors, though they may require assistance from shamans to find the right place. Spirits, including ancestral spirits, encountered in other dimensions, sometimes may be helpful and at other times harmful. The shaman has both to coax and to confront spirits, risking mental health and physical life in such fights. Sometimes spirits demand to be appeased by the sacrifice of animals. For instance, the 'black' shamans of the Yakut people of Siberia sacrificed black horses before the onset of winter.

As they have to outwit spirits, shamans are often tricksters. They may be so aware of their role as performers that they fake phenomena in order to awe and to entertain their audience. Their rituals help to reinforce their communities' social bonds. Indeed, all group rituals help to remind members of the group of their shared identity.

Some scholars claim that the mystic traditions of all the major faiths came from shamanic visions, as may well be the case with the description of the formation of our Matrix in the original text. Shamanic visions may be the source of heaven and hell as well, because shamans have to travel across landscapes both beautiful and nightmarish, whether they journey in their imaginations or far beyond them. Each shamanic tradition has its own descriptions of the upper worlds and the underworlds. For example, the Evenk, from whose language the word 'shaman' is derived, see three levels above this world and three below it, while the Yakut see one level above and one below. However hellish the underworlds, and however heavenly the upper worlds appear, the shamanic worldview tends towards the unity of the whole. The other worlds interlock with this world and an action in one has repercussions in another.

Many shamanic cultures distinguish between the shamans who journey in states of altered consciousness and the priests who do not. Pre-literate societies had priests and priestesses, but quite how they served their deities and their communities is a matter of speculation. As stated in the previous section, it is most likely that they performed rituals to mark the seasonal changes and the agricultural round, to placate the powers of nature or to ask for favours in the future.

The powers of nature, such as thunder, manifest, sometimes dramatically, in this world. They can also be met on shamanic journeys, or 'seen' with inner vision and perhaps clairvoyance. Over time, the powers of nature may become personified. A recent example is death, which has become 'personified' as Death, the scythe-wielding skeleton. As the forces of nature became personified into goddesses and gods, they acquired human and superhuman characteristics in the stories told about them. Respect and veneration changed subtly into worship. Religions became institutionalised with the building of huge temples, like the ziggurats of Mesopotamia, which dominated the land around them.

As new religions arose in the Middle East and spread from there, religious practices that preceded them were either absorbed or demonised.

An example of absorption is the Catholic feast day of St Brigid, which is celebrated on 1st February to mark the start of spring. The saint is thought to have been born around 450 CE in Ireland, the daughter of a Celtic chieftain and a Christian slave. She died in 526 CE after a life of good works, including giving much of her father's wealth to the poor. Her saint's day coincides with the Celtic festival of Imbolc, held to celebrate the start of spring and dedicated to the goddess Brid, also known as Brigid, the maiden aspect of the goddess.

The goddess Brid was demoted to the status of a saint, but Mary, the mother of Jesus, was elevated to the role of

Queen of Heaven, which was an epithet of Isis in Egypt, and of Nin-anna in Sumer. As Asherah or Astarte, the goddess was also at times hailed as the consort of the Hebrew god, which outraged the Hebrew prophets, including Jeremiah. Mary is usually portrayed as the loving mother and intercessor, but Isis, Nin-anna or Inanna and Astarte were complex figures, more like real women.

So many aspects of Christianity are borrowed from earlier solar cults, such as those of Orpheus and Attis, that the case can be made that it too is a solar cult without historical basis. For example, Christmas coincides neatly with the rebirth of the sun in northern latitudes at the winter solstice and the twelve disciples may represent the twelve signs of the zodiac.

Absorption of older religions by newer one can pose theologians with almost irreconcilable opposites. Gods are simultaneously vengeful and loving. In most creeds there comes a point where believers are expected to accept these apparent contradictions in faith.

As an example of demonization, the Greek Septuagint and the Latin Vulgate translation of Psalm 95 verse 5 reads, 'all the gods of the gentiles are devils.' A more accurate translation of the Hebrew is: 'all the gods of the peoples are things of nought.'

Once evil was believed to be abroad in the world, women were deemed particularly prone to its temptations. This view of women prevailed in one of the earliest monotheistic religions, Zoroastrianism. As the worship of Ahura Mazda was the state religion of the Persian Empire, from around 550 BCE until Alexander the Great's conquest in 331 BCE, and again during the Sassanid era from 241 to 651 CE, Zoroastrianism influenced Judaism, Christianity and Islam. Its origins lie in the vision of a 30-year-old man, Zarathustri, who lived sometime between 1500 and 1200 BCE. He placed the one creator god, Ahura Mazda, as the source of light above this world. In this world, the source of misery and evil, Angra Mainyu, took particular pleasure in war and strife. Eventually Ahura Mazda will overcome Angra Mainyu. In the meanwhile, believers had to try to be good in thought, word and deed, because after death the good will be greeted by a fair maiden, while the bad will be met by a foul-smelling hag. They will reside in a kind of heaven or a kind of hell until Ahura Mazda finally defeats evil. Thereafter, a second judgement will be passed on the spirits of the dead that will be binding for eternity.

One way to shield women from temptation was for their fathers, brothers and husbands to monitor their behaviour, which tied in neatly with the patriarchal family structures upon which rulers relied. Zoroastrianism expected women to revere their husbands, and insisted that menstruating women should keep their distance from pure elements like fire and water, as well as from other people.

With Zoroastrianism, the crystallisation of the harmful, malefic or demonic spirits, known to shamans, into the forces of evil seems complete. As discussed above, old gods are absorbed or demonised by the earthly representatives of the new ones. It is a useful rallying cry for any group to call its enemies' beliefs and practices evil, especially when priests and kings claim to speak with the authority of the gods. Such rallying cries were made by Pope Urban II in 1095 to launch the First Crusade. The consequences of western Christendom's encounters with Islam during Crusades affect the world to this day.

In their early stages, the major faiths all taught that women are spiritually as able as men to live in accordance with their teachings, but long practice has tended to work out differently.

**HINDUISM**[13] is based on the Vedas, which were first written down around 1500 BCE, when the Aryan people came into the Indian sub-continent from what is now Iran in the northwest. Like the original text of this book, the Vedas came from a long oral tradition. According to the Vedas, all other deities are manifestations of the one divine principle Brahma, and human life is a cycle of birth, death and rebirth, from which liberation or *moksha* can only be achieved through knowledge, devotion or action. Rebirth as a woman was sometimes considered a sign of wrongdoing in a previous life.

In the early centuries of Hinduism in India, worship took place in homes and women's role in ritual was deemed as essential as men's. Gradually, temples replaced homes as places of worship and priests came to officiate over more complicated rituals. Between 800 BCE and 400 BCE, teachings from the texts, known as the Upanishads, began to emphasize the ascetic path of learning. Both of these developments restricted women's participation.

Then, a priest called Manu laid out the caste system, in which only males from the highest Brahmin caste could achieve *moksha*. Consigning women of all castes to the control of their husbands and fathers, Manu also warned that a man who had intercourse with a menstruating woman risked losing his vitality, energy, wisdom, strength and sight. To this day many women do not enter temples during their periods.

Inherently wild, wicked and impure, because of their biology, women were exhorted in many texts to subdue their nature by being subservient wives and selflessly devoted mothers. Only then could they be considered virtuous. Nevertheless, a girl's first period was, and is, celebrated with gifts and where it occurs, seclusion during menstruation is regarded as a time for women to rest. It is only comparatively recently those Hindu women have begun to escape from male control by working independently outside the home.

In some of the many goddess cults within Hinduism, temples are reserved for women only. The idol of Parvati, at the Chengannur Mahadeva temple in Kerala, is said to menstruate occasionally and when she does, a special ceremony, called *thripootherattu,* is held on the fourth day of her period. The reverence of men and women, for goddesses, does not necessarily equate with any degree of equality in the home.

Among the Hindu sects are Tantra and Shaktism; the origins of both may pre-date the Vedas, though Shaktism began between the 4th century and 7th century CE, and Tantra between the 5th century and the 9th century CE. The central deities are Shakti or Parvati, her incarnations as Kali and Durga, and her consort Shiva. Without Shakti, Shiva is powerless, because Shakti, as the divine mother, demands complete surrender. In the paintings depicting the god's surrender to the goddess, she stands or sits clothed and fully armed on his body, which lies naked, either on the ground, or on her throne with more gods below them. The goddess has between four and 20 arms, in which she holds weapons and other devices to show her authority, power and control. The consort has two arms and holds nothing. He is content to be her provider and servant. In other paintings, the goddess is shown killing the demons that resist her authority.

In Shaktism, no distinction is drawn between spirit and matter, so the latter is regarded as creative rather than as a snare and delusion. Associated in the West with sexual techniques to enhance pleasure, Tantra is, in fact, more concerned with weaving all the threads of a life in the patterns set by nature. Sexual union, especially when the woman is menstruating, can be part of the path to union with the divine, but so too can the extreme asceticism of the *sadhu,* who renounces material life to meditate in solitude. An important element of Tantra is raising the *kundalini* energy, which in most people lies dormant, coiled like a serpent at the base of the spine. Those who can raise the *kundalini* have powers and perceptions beyond the norm, which may be why Tantra is associated with black magic. When the energetic channel that lets the *kundalini* rise up the spine is blocked, the individual concerned becomes unhinged and sometimes dies. The serpent energy is dangerous and most yoga practices are intended to clear the channel just in case the *kundalini* rises accidentally.

JUDAISM's roots go back approximately 3800 years to the time of Abraham. Although classical rabbinical Judaism dates only from the 1st century BCE, Moses may have lived around 3,500 years ago, and the Book of

Genesis was probably written in the 6<sup>th</sup> century or 5<sup>th</sup> century BCE.

The idea that Eve came from Adam's rib, may be a reference back to Ninti, but the pun that worked in Sumerian does not work in Hebrew. Where Ninti means both *lady of the rib* and *lady of life,* Eve means *life-giver*. The Semitic word for Adam, the original man, is derived from *adama*, which means *soil*. As everything which humans need to feed, clothe and shelter us comes from the soil, what does that suggest about man's original purpose? Could it be that Adam, and all the men after him, were meant to take on the role of the soil by supporting and supplying women?

Genesis describes Eve as Adam's helper. In Semitic languages, there are two words for helper. One is used for a subordinate who helps a superior, while the other is used when a superior helps a subordinate. In Hebrew, the word for the second kind of helper is *ezer*. This is the word used to describe Eve.

The roots of *ezer* are *-z-r*, which means *to rescue* or *to save*, and *g-z-r*, which means *to be strong*. The two words became conflated, because, in modern Hebrew, *g* at the start of a word is not sounded, but neither meaning indicates inferiority. As Hebrew is written without vowels, *ezer* is also related to the older word *azar,* which means *to surround*, but *azar* also carries the meanings of *to protect, to aid* and *to succour*. This meaning may explain why some English translations refer to Eve as being Adam's helpmate.

*Ezer* is used 21 times in the Old Testament. Usually, as in Psalms 115, 121 and 124, it describes the power and the role of the Lord rather than of Eve, which makes its use in connection with her highly significant.

The story in the Book of Genesis continues with Eve's seduction by the serpent, which is a discreet reference to male genitals. The Christians turned Eve's encounter with the serpent as her fall into original sin, and her ability to give spiritual life by biological birth was twisted into the curse of labour for all women.

Judaism is primarily concerned with working out the covenant their god made with his chosen people in this world. Jewish history contains stories of strong women who were familiar with the scriptures and laws, and who sometimes opposed male leaders.

In early Judaism, women were exempted from religious observance because they were deemed innately spiritual. Men were considered so innately unspiritual that they had to practise their devotions. Women remain exempt from all religious observance except the laws regarding menstruation, childbirth and diet. Marriage was, and still is, based on companionship rather than procreation, and women cannot be married without their consent. Jews have never sought converts and only the children of Jewish mothers are recognized as Jewish.

Like other religions, Judaism contains distinct, sometimes argumentative, sects. In the mystical traditions of the Kabbalah, the female aspect of the one god is honoured as the *Shekinah,* who dwells in the west. Those of the priest caste who claim descent through the male line from Moses' brother Aaron, who are aged between 15 and 55 and without physical or spiritual blemish, face the *Shekinah* in the west to recite one particular blessing.

Based on the experience and teachings of Gautama Buddha, **BUDDHISM** began in the 5th century BCE. Buddhism states that all humans can achieve enlightenment regardless of gender or caste.

Enlightenment is the escape from the cycle of suffering through life, death and rebirth in the world of *maya* or illusion. It is attainable by acknowledging the Four Noble Truths and following the Eight Fold Path. However, Theravada Buddhism teaches that enlightenment is only possible for those who adopt the monastic life, while Mahayana Buddhism maintains it is attainable more easily, but not exclusively, by those in monasteries than by those who lead an ordinary life.

The Four Noble Truths examine the nature of suffering in this impermanent, imperfect world. Our bodies cause suffering and so do our minds, greedy for and clinging to temporary satisfactions. All suffering stems from the illusion of separation, a sentiment with which the original writers would have concurred. Detachment from desire leads to the end of suffering and the achievement of *nirvana,* or freedom from desire. The way to nirvana is the middle course, between self-indulgence and extreme asceticism. In this view of the world, gods and devils are redundant, because suffering is self-inflicted and gradually released through an individual's lifetimes through the workings of cause and effect or *karma*.

Buddhism has a Tantric variant, which, like Hindu Tantra, acknowledges the indivisibility of spirit and matter. The world is consciousness at play. Enlightenment is the realization that all that exists is divine. Within Buddhist Tantra, there is the 'left-hand' path of sexual techniques that facilitate enlightenment, but these are only one part of the whole.

As Buddhism spread across Asia, it came into areas where the family structure was already patriarchal and it did not challenge the status quo. There are no doctrinal restrictions placed on women when they menstruate, as it is regarded as natural. However, in some areas, women are not permitted to enter temples during their periods. The orders of nuns have been subordinated to the orders of monks, so that a senior nun is expected to defer to a junior monk.

The replacement of BC and AD by BCE (before common era) and CE (common era) masks but does not hide the dating of the start of **CHRISTIANITY** to the year zero.

Entry into the Christian Church is through baptism to which women have the same access as men.

In the early years of Christianity, women could become apostles, prophets and deacons. Both sexes continued to have the same rights and duties for a while, perhaps until the 4th century CE when Christianity became the official religion of the Roman Empire.

The recognition of Christianity by the Roman Empire resulted in the suppression of other forms of religious practice, including the celebration of women's mysteries.

Based on the rape of Persephone by her uncle Hades, the lord of the underworld, and her mother Demeter's frantic search for her, the mysteries were celebrated in classical Greece and in areas of Greek influence. The rituals of descent, search and rebirth may have involved the use of hallucinogenic drugs. These experiential, essentially feminine mysteries were markedly different to the male dominated religions. The celebration of the mysteries at Eleusis, near Athens, entered the historical record in a Homeric Hymn around 650 BCE. The rites at Eleusis were banned in 392 CE and the temple was sacked by Alaric the Goth four years later. Given that the rites were celebrated regularly for over 1,000 years, it is quite remarkable how many initiates, who included Roman emperors as well as women and slaves, obeyed the injunction to keep silent. Although Apuleius hints at the nature of the rites at the Temple of Isis towards the end of his *Metamorphoses*, also called *The Golden Ass,* written around 170 CE, no accurate description of the rites is known.

Once established as the Roman Empire's official religion, Christianity started to equate Rome's patriarchal social structures with divine law. For centuries afterwards, women were expected to be obedient to male rule.

One particular doctrine, that of original sin, was cited in the western churches — Catholic and Protestant — as reinforcement for female obedience. First alluded to by Irenaeus, Bishop of Lyon in the third century, the doctrine of original sin was expanded by Augustine of Hippo (354-430) so that blame for the fall of man rested on Eve, and therefore on all women, This doctrine influenced the western churches until the 20$^{th}$ century, although Orthodox Christianity has viewed the fall rather differently.

Orthodox Christianity expects women to refrain from communion during menstruation, but other restrictions are absent from almost all denominations.

When **ISLAM** was introduced in the 7th century CE, the lives of women in the Arabian Peninsula improved. Women were expected to honour the Five Pillars as men were, they not only attended the mosques, they led in worship and had a religious education. Female infanticide was banned, and women were better protected in matters of marriage and inheritance. Mohammed's first wife Khadija, a merchant in her own right, was hugely supportive of him and, after his death, his widows, particularly Aisha, were involved in teaching Islam.[14]

As Islam spread, religious power was concentrated in the hands of priests who were able to enforce codes of public modesty more and more strictly, until women were confined to the homes of their fathers or husbands. Yet again, patriarchal social structures, which controlled women, were given religious legitimacy.

In Islam, menstruation is regarded as a nuisance, during which a woman may not enter a mosque and after which she may take a ritual bath, like Jewish women.

Islam teaches that everything comes from Allah, and what is deemed evil is either natural, as in the disasters caused by floods or earthquakes, or caused by disobedience to the divine will. However, along with humanity, Allah created angels and djinns, including Iblis. Whereas angels do not have the free will to sin, the djinns whisper in people's ears to tempt them into transgressions against the laws of Islam.

\*\*\*\*\*

Individual women of all five faiths have led, and continue to lead, lives of great goodness and charity. They have found, and continue to find, consolation in their religion. This is beyond question.

However, women of faith have also had to contend with vitriolic condemnations of their gender as lustful or unclean, in the texts of most religions throughout the ages. By and large, women have accepted the lower status allotted to them by their religion, without realizing how much power they have conceded.

Over the centuries, men too have conceded power to priests. Once priests claimed they were the only ones able to interpret the commands of the deity, they alone spoke for and on behalf of the divine. Particularly in Christianity, they have become the arbiters of good and evil, able to hold out the promise of paradise to the virtuous and the threat of eternal punishment to the sinful. The possibility of rewards in the afterlife, of the life everlasting and of the chance of rebirth, is so hugely attractive that many believers are not concerned by the degree of authority that they have handed over to their priests.

In most faiths, the priests are predominantly male, and so comparatively few men are able to control vast numbers of men and women. If you need to be convinced that organized religions are organs of control, look at the wealth they accumulate and how they use it.

Moreover, consider how religions cause suffering, from the individual, private agonies of conscience, to full-scale wars over doctrinal differences. Wars have been fought by members of every single one of the six major faiths against at least one of the others. The sects within religions have also fought each other. For example, Catholics have fought the Orthodox and the Protestants. Sunnis have fought Shias. Religions are at their most dangerous when environmental harshness combines with political instability and economic inequalities, to feed fundamentalist interpretations of the holy books and to justify conflict.

Overall, religions endorse the rights of men to control women, not least by legitimizing the position of men as heads of families.

## A MAD WORLD, MY MASTERS[15]

Again it must be stressed that individual men are not to blame for the existence or power of the patriarchy. Men have suffered as much as women under the male domination that stems from the fundamental disconnectedness of the Y chromosome. They have fought the battles and suffered from the physical and emotional injuries of war. They have had to compete for their place in the hierarchy. Those who reach the top have often become suspicious and paranoid. Those trapped at the bottom, and unable to provide for those they care for, feel like failures. As big boys are not supposed to cry, from childhood, males have been cut off from their feelings, and as adults can find it difficult to express emotions and to relate to other people.

Language is an insidious form of patriarchal control. We have been fed messages by men and by women who support the patriarchy, as well as by ourselves. All our lives, we have been told we are too much this, not enough that. We have been taught to know our place in the scheme of things. Boys learn fairly young that, however low their status is, that of girls is lower, because the language we use makes masculine behaviours and characteristics seem normal, while feminine behaviours and characteristics appear aberrant.

Add to language the images from advertising, blockbuster films and pornography, and it becomes clear why so many men feel entitled to the sexual and domestic servitude of women.

Now consider how the structures of the fear-based patriarchy have defined and affected you.

We have evolved into such separate creatures that too many of us live isolated, lonely lives, obsessed by the desperate struggle to survive. Our isolation and desperation happen to suit those who have power and control over the vast majority of us very well. They are the most entrenched of the patriarchs, whose rule rests of the use or threat of force.

As a study of dictatorships shows, the individual who wins and can keep the support of a few well-armed and vicious thugs, is able to enforce his (almost invariably his) rule over large numbers of people. An example of how a ruthless man is able to exercise power over others may be seen in Kenneth Branagh's performance in the 2001 film, *Conspiracy*. Branagh played the role of Heydrich, the senior Nazi officer who exploited his rank, his mastery of detail and the threat of force, to initiate the Final Solution to the Third Reich's 'Jewish problem'.

At every level from vast empires to intimate families, men have exercised control over other men and women because they have, or can call on, the physical strength to do so.

The patriarchy's reliance on force to keep, or gain control over, the planet's resources means that the military consumes a significant proportion of said resources, a great deal of human ingenuity and huge amounts of money. According to the Stockholm International Peace Research Institute, the figures in billions of US dollars for defence spending in 2010 were 698 by the USA, 119 by China, 59.6 by the UK, 59.3 by France and 58.7 by Russia.[16]

The statistics on domestic violence are horrible. In 2012, figures estimated that one in four women in the UK experiences domestic violence at least once in her lifetime. One in six men in the UK experiences domestic violence at least once in his lifetime.

The patriarchy extends beyond the family and religion into economics. Given how scathing the original writers were about religions, what would they have made of global corporate capitalism? It depends on endless growth on a planet with finite resources, on demands that outstrip supply, on competition for resources and on money, most of which exists only on computerized spread sheets.[17]

Corporate capitalism's emphasis on competitiveness makes for division and separation, for success and failure, for winners and losers. The drive towards globalization concentrates power and wealth in the hands of a few at the expense of the many. In 2011, the protesters, who camped out on Wall Street in New York and in other cities, became known as the Occupy movement. Occupy claimed that the world's wealth is held by a mere 1% of the population. Some of the 1 % realize that their riches isolate them from genuine community, the rest regard themselves as insulated from the economic woes of the 99%.

The global corporate conspiracy makes it acceptable for 12% of the world's population to be obese through over-eating, while a similar percentage goes to sleep hungry every night.[18]

Whether or not it is deliberate policy, global capitalism eats into the lands that are home to the world's few remaining indigenous peoples. At the very least, these peoples used to know how to live lightly and their elders hold much spiritual wisdom that the rest of humanity has lost.

All fear-based attempts to control the uncontrollable are folly, because **structures that go against the natural flow of the energy through the World of Interactions are doomed to fail sooner or later. All attempts to control women and the cycles of nature go against the flow of the Matrix and are** doomed to fail. All patriarchal structures go against the flow of the Matrix will therefore fail.

For those willing to see, the cracks in all patriarchal structures – families, religions, governments, banks and corporations — are obvious.

## SCIENCE

When people say that science is the new religion, perhaps they are more accurate than they realize, for, like religions, science is riddled with sects, orthodoxies and power-hungry individuals. For example, anyone who questions the current orthodoxy, that climate change is caused by human activity, is liable to personal as well as professional attack. Challenges to any doctrine are ignored and then ridiculed, before they are seriously considered and are given the chance to become the next orthodoxy.

Some ideas are in vogue; others are not. For instance, the theories of Nikola Tesla and the practical applications of his work, which could be useful in solving the energy crisis, are anathema to grant providing bodies and, therefore, to many universities as well.

Increasingly, the sciences are coming under the control of the global corporations, which fund research and steer the directions in which it goes. Pharmaceutical companies, for example, are more interested in treating patients for as long as possible, than in their recovery. There is less profit in actually curing patients.

The writers of the original texts foresaw the possibility of the evolution of 'techno-sapiens', thinking machines.

Transhumanism has become the subject of serious intellectual debate since the 1960s, as technological developments make possible the physical and intellectual enhancement of the human body and the creation of artificial intelligence. The potential for both organic and inorganic improvements makes transhumanism attractive in many ways. Health is better, youth and life are extended and where silicon replaces carbon, beings may exist without messy bodily functions, uncomfortable emotions, illnesses and physical deaths. Where Gilgamesh failed to defeat sleep, let alone death, transhumanists see strong possibility.

Since the novel, *Frankenstein,* was first published in 1818, science fiction has portrayed transhumanism's utopian and dystopian potentials. The ethical dilemmas it poses are considerable. Where it seeks to control life, transhumanism echoes the patriarchy. Although it looks to technological developments to alleviate individual and collective suffering, many of the new technologies will be available only to the wealthy, because of the costs of research and production.

One of the arguments in and against the transhumanist movement is the idea of playing god. (On a flippant note, would 'techno-sapiens' send their error reports to the great god of computers in the sky or to their mythical forefathers St Bill Gates and St Steve Jobs?) More seriously, would 'techno-sapiens', created by us and able to supersede us, serve the evolutionary process of the Matrix towards full realisation of unity? On the other hand, the Matrix does not care how we evolve. It exists only to allow for the evolution of consciousness.

By applying the viewpoint of the original text to transhumanism, it seems to leave out the levels of consciousness that lie latent in most of us. Already accessible to shamans and mystics, these levels can be reached by anyone prepared to devote time and energy to spiritual development.

Levels of consciousness wider than the norm are also accessible to highly trained soldiers. There is a strange area where the occult, technology and the military, meet the global corporate élite and possibly some of the weirder manifestations of the Matrix. It contains and extends past ufology. Its shadowy, multi-layered existence is suggested by the claims and counter-claims of those who leak stories of participation in odd kinds of research and activities, of those who tell of their abduction experiences, and of those who research conspiracies. You venture down that particular rabbit hole at your peril, for it stretches the bounds of your beliefs and challenges your concepts of history and present reality.[17]

Serious study of consciousness, which draws together neuro-science, psychology and philosophy, is already happening in Russia and elsewhere. Prioritizing this research, by bringing it further into the public domain and funding it without expectation of commercial return, could well prove to be a wiser investment in the future of humanity than the billions currently spent on weapons, allopathic drugs and genetic modification. The science of consciousness may well be able to explain how the ancients moved the massive blocks of stone at Baalbek and built the pyramids at Giza. It is equally likely to offer solutions to many of the world's current ills.

Meanwhile, scientific research is mainly still tied to the mechanistic ideas of cause and effect developed by Rene Descartes and Isaac Newton in the 16th century and 17th century. Year by year, even month by month, what was in the realm of fiction enters our reality. In less than three decades, technologies have transformed the ways in which we connect with each other and with our world. The benefits are so obvious that we overlook who developed the technologies and why. The development of the internet, for example, was driven mainly by the military, pornographers and powerbrokers, who manipulate and control public opinion. What connects us in new ways is also what divides and separates us in new ways.

The lure of the newest shiniest gadgets obscures the extent to which we conform to their systems. Increasingly we are accepting information in digital form. As our bodies are carbon-based, we prefer information that is presented to us in analogue form, such as the hands on a traditional clock face, illustrations and charts. Our brains look for patterns and we can recognize people whom we have seen before, even when they are only partially visible. But the pattern recognition that is easy for humans is difficult to programme into silicon-based computers which process data in digital form in columns of numbers. We have become so familiar with the letters and figures on digital display boards that we do not think about why they have to be presented in those shapes.

Computerized systems can process information so fast that the human operator is seen as the limiting factor. For example, the on-board computers in modern aircraft can override some of the pilots' decisions, although not vice versa.

As was mentioned in the section on emergent behaviour, software can be designed so that the bytes of information swarm to fulfil the goal set by the programmer, and sometimes the results are not the ones anticipated. It is more than possible that new combinations of hardware and software will evade human control and start to develop according to their own needs and capabilities. Without minds, they will not be alive, but they could become a menace.

Knowledge, it is said, is power. These days, we concede power not only to machines but also to those who can access the information in them. Security and speed cameras track our movements; most of our money exists only in the data bases that record our financial transactions; our communications are monitored by web spiders so that we can be fed adverts; our preferences are noted so that politicians can persuade us to vote for them, and our votes are registered or counted mechanically. These are just some of the ways in which we have given control of our lives to machines and, therefore, to the organizations that own and operate them. Think what power the Stasi or the KGB would have had if they had had access to the kind of data banks that are available now.

Databases have an error rate of between plus or minus five and plus or minus seven per cent. For those of us innocently going about our business, computer errors are a nuisance. For those whom the authorities suspect of wrongdoing, computer errors can be fatal. Think of the drones that are used to drop bombs and the mistakes that have been made.

Science and technology have their own momentum. As with the development of the atomic and hydrogen bombs in the 1940s, the fact that human ingenuity can invent something does not mean it is the wise or best thing to make and use.

## SUFFERING

Suffering is an inescapable part of being human. You cannot and will never control the natural processes to which you and every human are subject. You have been born with a body and your body will inevitably die, and while you live in your body, your life is utterly dependent on the planet. The bodies of the people you love die too and you mourn their passing.

We have come to believe that understanding and wisdom may be achieved only through suffering, as if it tempers us as heat tempers steel. Religions have endorsed the idea that suffering ennobles us. Painful experiences can indeed be spurs to self-discovery, but they can also warp us when we individually or collectively armour ourselves against possible future hurt and losses.

The whole patriarchal system can be seen as an attempt to armour and protect the powerful against suffering. Patriarchal structures promote selfishness and separation and cause more suffering. The tragedy is that in to tolerating the patriarchy, we turn a blind eye to the harm done to the vulnerable and powerless.

We suffer too because we judge others and ourselves.

## JUDGEMENT

Although the original writers were well aware of the absurdity of making any absolute statement, they were clear that there are no absolutes. Without the existence of a creator god, there is no ultimate judge of right and wrong. Indeed, one reason why humans created gods was to establish them as the arbiters of good and evil. In the name of the gods, horrible punishments have been meted out to heretics and transgressors. Maybe worse still, the invention of gods has allowed priests to make a false division of the energy of the whole into spirit and matter.

All human values are relative, for one creed's definition of right and wrong is often rather different to another's. Moses' Ten Commandments read differently in Hebrew than in the English of the King James Bible. The latter says, 'Thou shalt not kill,' but the former says, 'No murder.'

In hierarchical thinking, all qualities associated with good are placed above those associated with evil. Where good is associated with positive, male, light and white, evil is associated with negative, female, dark and black, so white and male join good on top, and black and female join evil on the bottom.

English translations of the I Ching, the Chinese Book of Changes, certainly make such associations: the firm lines are positive, male, strong and great, while the broken lines are negative, female, weak and small. In view of this, it is all the more surprising that Hexagram 11, in which three broken lines representing earth are above three strong lines representing heaven, is called *Tai* and means *peace*, while Hexagram 12, in which heaven is over earth, is called *P'i* and means *stagnation* or *obstruction*.

Positive qualities are admired while negative qualities are shunned. When conscious and rational are seen as positive, they join male at the top of the hierarchy. When unconscious and irrational are associated with female, they are relegated to the bottom.

As judgements are rooted in hierarchical thinking, all judgements made on the basis of hierarchical (and usually unconscious) associations serve to maintain the status quo. They also lead to many forms of discrimination and suffering.

The Tao Te Ching, the summation of Lao Tse's philosophy, comments in Chapter 38 on what happens when judgements of right and wrong become more important than following the Tao, the Way. When the wholeness of the Tao is lost, there is a descent through goodness, kindness and justice to the emptiness of ritual and finally to confusion.

The original text said something similar. Only that which flows with the Matrix is sustainable. Everything that is out of the flow of the Matrix is doomed to fail.

The yin yang symbol depicts the balance between two equal and interdependent forces that together make a whole. The wise person walks the line between them, in the knowledge that the light (and everything associated with the light), will never overcome the dark (and everything associated with the dark), because both together make the unity.

The hierarchy of judgement can be turned through ninety degrees to become the horizontal line of *both – and*, rather than vertical line of *either/or*. The process of shifting from the vertical to the horizontal begins with the acceptance of the interconnectedness of all. It is a vital stage in rendering male energy, which tends to separation, compatible with female energy, which tends to relatedness.

Changing from *either/or* to *both – and* helps you to accept all the aspects of yourself that you do not like, or in Jungian terms to integrate your shadow. When you live in an interconnected world, you know that you too are capable of any act a human can do. You are capable of committing atrocities, because people are, and, importantly, you choose not to commit such acts, because what hurts another hurts you.

Your behaviour is based on the so-called Golden Rule, 'Do as you would be done by.' This principle not only has a long history, it was also found in many cultures from ancient Egypt to China. Confucius advised people not to impose on others what they would hate themselves.

'Do as you would be done by,' instead of doing as you have been done by, is important for every woman who receives a man's surrender. Male surrender is not meant to be the opposite of the usual model of male control. It is intended to be liberation from old roles, for both men and women.

## THE THIRD OPTION

In addition to the two concepts of *either/or* and *both – and*, there is always the third option.

When a sales assistant offers you the choice between the hardback edition of a book or the paperback, you can exercise the third option — not to buy either. Real free will is to walk away from making a choice at all, provided that you accept full responsibility for so doing.

Defenders of global capitalism point their detractors to the failure of communism and declare that no other economic system works. There is actually a third option that has not yet been tried — a system that conserves irreplaceable resources and ensures the fairer distribution of food and other necessities.

'Third option' economics will emerge in our world once enough people accept the interconnectedness of all things and the powerful force that is love.

## LOVE

This is not a word that the original writers used in any of its many meanings, other than to question the concept of gods that love humanity. It is a word too glibly used by the Christian churches, New Agers and romantic fiction writers.

Love is much more than most people conceive it to be.

And it is the strongest force in a universe created by the desire of the ____/N-One-ness to become conscious of itself.

Love unifies and honours the unity of all creation.

Love is the transformative energy that accepts and surrenders to all the processes of life.

Love is the open-handed opposite of the fear that clenches the fist.

But love can be invoked to justify many forms of control. In its name the priests and patriarchs constrict behaviour, as does the Bitch Goddess.

## THE BITCH GODDESS

Between the patriarchy and a world led by women, towers the archetypal figure of the Bitch Goddess. She is the Snow Queen in Hans Christian Andersen's story and Jadis in C.S.Lewis's *The Lion, The Witch and The Wardrobe*. She is the being that Galadriel feared to become if she accepted the ring from Frodo, in *The Lord of the Rings*. She is Kali and Sekhmet when they kill both the wicked and the righteous. She is Ninhursag, enraged enough to send the wasting disease to Enki.

As with goddesses, so with women. They are loving and nurturing *and* they are passionate and sexual *and* they are capable of anger, righteous and otherwise, and of killing. They can and do manifest the Bitch Goddess who lusts for life and devours it. This archetype is a force to be reckoned with and she is never, ever, reasonable.

Born in the gulf between men and women, the Bitch Goddess consumes the energy of the patriarchy's attempts to control women. She lurks in every woman who lashes out, yells, scorns, complains, criticizes, withholds and manipulates, through her sexual desirability, or her role as wife or mother. She lurks behind every man who lashes out, yells, scorns, complains, criticizes, withholds and manipulates, through sexuality and his role as father or husband. She is the sum total of human projections and assumptions, jealousies and fears about the wild side of women.

One of her easiest targets is male virility. Men's insecurities about their performance and about being 'found out', make them particularly sensitive and vulnerable about their role as lovers. This is why, in so many cultures, men have tried to insist that their brides are virgins, and why sexually experienced women are labelled whores. (This is somewhat ironic because prostitutes are paid to flatter men rather than complain, like their wives.) For both men and women, sexual frustration is probably the main reason why the Bitch Goddess erupts.

Women can be so scared by the wildness and lack of reasonableness of the Bitch Goddess that, when they find her in themselves, or in others, they prefer male control. It seems safer than giving vent to the Bitch Goddess in any of her guises. Her raw potential is particularly strong in menstruating, menopausal and post-menopausal women. At these stages in a woman's life, it is helpful to her, and to the people around her, if she is approached with respectful recognition of her power.

When the Bitch Goddess fully expresses herself, she may be cold as stone or a raging torrent, like a river in spate. More often, she is muted, so that she complains and nags until she repels lovers, children and friends. Such losses frustrate her so that complaints become self-fulfilling.

Terrible as they are, in all her aspects the Bitch Goddess has something important to say. She knows what is wrong in her world and, actively or passively, she is aggressive in saying it. Therein lies the problem with her. Her aggression triggers the fight or flight response in those around her, because they do not react to what she is saying, but to how she says it.

Her message is usually this: her needs are not being met. When she feels too disempowered to meet her needs herself, she must rely on others, and she borrows the patriarchal model of *power over* to try to get her own way. When she demands more and more things, she is still caught up in materialism, because the things she says she wants are symbolic of deeper, inexpressible needs, such as (self)-acceptance.

Sometimes when the Bitch Goddess rages, she is also warning people. She reminds humanity that the laws of nature are inviolable. The cycle of growth begins with seeding and ends in fruiting. The harvest is followed by decay and death. The land must rest until it is time for the new seeds to sprout. Knowing that death is necessary and inevitable, she exposes the myth of endless growth. She is clear that, unchecked by female authority, males who use their spiritual energy for, and by themselves, are capable of doing something as stupid as drilling a hole in the bottom of a boat or sawing off the branch they are sitting on.

The rage of the Bitch Goddess over the exploitation of the feminine principle, of the earth, of women and of children is useful fuel to power the change of consciousness necessary to heal rifts.

For her real message to be received, the Bitch Goddess must not be fought, because the battle escalates until one party or the other is annihilated. She pursues those who try to flee from her, so running away from her is pointless.

She cannot communicate aggressively, to ensure her real message is heard, she has to be assertive instead.

The slight, but crucial, difference between aggression and assertiveness is illustrated by the reactions of dogs. As pack animals, they look to a leader, canine or human. In the absence of a leader, dogs fight for dominance. Shouting angrily at a disobedient dog does not work: the shouting human is just another dog fighting for leadership of the pack. Telling the dog to sit clearly and firmly, usually does work, because the human is asserting the right to lead.

The Bitch Goddess wants nothing less than surrender. Then, and only then, is she disarmed as surely as Shiva stopped Kali's killing spree by incarnating as a helpless child. Male surrender is neither flight nor fright. It is the acknowledgement by men that the Bitch Goddess's grievances are legitimate. In order to surrender, men must share her grief. Surrender is not temporary appeasement. When men sympathize for the moment and then revert to their old habits of thought and behaviour, the Bitch Goddess is stirred to greater rage.

Women start to disarm the Bitch when they see and hear her as a symbol of their disempowerment. It is not easy to cast off the shackles of male control, to drop ingrained reactions to frustration, or to stop the subtle manipulation of others, but a huge step along the path is to accept and integrate the most important idea presented in this book. Connected to the fabric of the Matrix in ways that men are not and cannot be, women are better equipped to lead humanity.

Women who are willing to disarm the Bitch are ready to accept male surrender.

## MALE SURRENDER

Many people are sincerely dedicated to healing the planet. To one degree or another, they have worked on themselves; they have recognized the pain and the rage; they follow the path of the Goddess. They try to be the change they want to make in the world; they see some of the current system's failures and speculate about adjustments to it. They are trying to mend something broken beyond repair, rather than leap into the unknown, in trust that a world led by women will work for the benefit of all.

A shift in mass consciousness is already perceptible to those sensitive to it. Many activists and bloggers see the weaknesses and follies of the patriarchal structures and predict its decline. Several bloggers describe their experiences of changes in subtle energies and write of the return of the divine feminine. However, very few people go as far as proposing the transfer of power from men to women, even though this will facilitate the emergence of a completely new system, that will serve life in all its myriad forms.

The main reason why the act of surrender by men, and the receiving of it by women, is so difficult is that it relies on trust. Men who are used to being in control, fear that if they concede power to women, then women will subject them to the same treatment that they have meted out for centuries. Despite the possibility that some women may seize the opportunity to exact revenge, the purpose of the transfer of power is to heal the damage caused by male control, not to perpetuate it by making men suffer. Women fear that if they take their innate power, they will become as hard and ruthless as men. Women also fear the responsibilities of power, because they will no longer be able to blame men.

There is a difference in quality between male control and female authority. In the original text, there is only one word to mean both authority and control, but the context makes the meaning clear. Male control has to be imposed from the top down, because men tend to think hierarchically. Women, who attain positions of power in male-controlled structures, have to exercise power within the hierarchy and, therefore, have to operate in much the same way as men, but female authority is actually different. It reflects the natural order, because it is, essentially, spiritual. When men elude female authority, their actions create more rifts and more suffering. When women use their authority, they make, and keep, men aware of, and compatible with, the female essence of the Matrix.

When the original writers described women as superior to men, they meant it spiritually as well as physically. (Remember that the fabric of the Matrix is general spiritual energy in dense form, and humans are a combination of general spiritual energy and individual energy.) In their view, the role of women is to create spiritually, as well as biologically, and so men's proper role was, is and always will be to serve, support and supply women, so that women can properly attend to their spiritual work. This is the opposite of patriarchal social structures, in which women attend to male needs ahead of their own.

Images of women as containers and men as pipes, rods or swords have an obvious anatomical source, but they also apply at the level of spiritual energy. If men pipe, or channel, their share of the general spiritual energy to women, then women can convert both their own spiritual energy, and that which they receive from males, into action in order to transform the World of Interactions The more energy men channel to women, the greater the changes women can accomplish for the mutual advantage of all.

The original writers offered another image for the process. The female spiritual principle is a bird and the male spiritual energy is her food. The better fed the bird is, the further she can fly.

The Shakhti and Tantric paintings, mentioned earlier, also illustrate the transfer of energy. The many-armed goddesses hold weapons of chastisement, but they also confer boons and blessings in exchange for the god's surrender of his power.

Male surrender begins with the recognition of the Bitch Goddess's grievances, as she acts as a gatekeeper to a different way of life. Once her threshold is crossed, surrender demands conscious, continuous and lasting effort for both men and women.

The text stressed that only women who are free of male control can receive men's surrender. The original writers referred to such women as goddesses. As the word *Goddess* has acquired layers of meaning from the religious to the sexual, the researcher and the editor have chosen to revive an archaic word: it is LIFEFUL. In addition to the obvious meaning, *full of life* or *animated*, lifeful also means *full of vitality* and, most significantly, *giving vitality to*.

Every woman who is free of male control is lifeful, for the same reasons that she is powerful. She is *in* the World of Interactions and *of* it. She listens to the intuitive voice of her heart and when she acts on her heart's guidance, she is in such harmony with the World of Interactions that she cannot make mistakes. No longer subject to man-made rules, she cannot do anything wrong and she cannot sin. She is lifeful, and the evolution of consciousness and conscious evolution of the Matrix, depends on her to be and to act. She has the right, and the duty, to exercise spiritual authority over males, to prevent them from doing further physical or emotional damage to themselves or to women. She has the right, and the duty, to use her ability to weave the fabric of the Matrix into the forms she chooses in order to alleviate suffering and to create the future.

If you are a woman, you may find it hard to believe that you cannot make mistakes. When you act from awareness of your connection to the fabric of the Matrix, you really are beyond judgement and in the place where there are no mistakes. Perhaps the only mistake you can make is not to take the risk of breaking away from male control.

At first, it is daunting to accept a man's surrender, to be in charge and to make all decisions. You can be and do anything you choose, and the surrendered man accepts, absorbs and supports you, and does your will at all times. You can rant and rave, because heartfelt rage is sometimes your only response to a crazy world; you can be affectionate; you can take the space to be alone and still the surrendered man is there for you.

The lifeful woman exercises her authority by knowing, beyond doubt, that she has the absolute right to do so. She is assertive, and while men fight or flee from female aggression, they are hard-wired to submit to female assertiveness.

If you are a woman, you may doubt that you can be assertive enough to be lifeful. The deeper the wounds inflicted on you by male and female representatives of the patriarchy, the more difficult it is likely to be for you to summon up the confidence to assert yourself. It might be helpful to think of a female role model. Perhaps you had a teacher who could silence a class with a raised eyebrow? Perhaps you have watched (maybe with a mixture of disapproval and admiration) an upper-class woman in a hotel, or at a shop counter, who gets her own way immediately, because it does not occur to her that she will not?

Assertiveness may sound similar to aggressiveness but it is very different in quality. When you are assertive, men submit. Your assertiveness tells them that you are confident and you know what you are doing and they no longer have to pretend that they understand the world. The original text states that all women need to assert their authority over all men in the full knowledge that they have the right to do so.

A surprising number of men actually want women to be assertive. They are convinced already that women are part of the planet in ways they are not and never can be. At home and at work, such men are happier under female authority. The researcher is sure that there are more men who want to be under female authority, than there are women willing to assert it, because women have been conditioned over centuries to deny their natural power. The researcher is also convinced that these men are far more likely to be alpha males, who know the hollowness of worldly success, than the sort of men who want women to mother them.

For a man who truly cares for a woman, submitting to her, and doing her will at all times, feels natural. It satisfies his yearning for connection and intimacy, because deep down, he knows that he has returned to the natural order. Surrender gives his actions purpose and brings meaning to his life. He escapes from traditional male roles, which are often enforced by peer pressure. Above all, he knows he cannot cause any more harm.

This form of relationship is not for wimps or mummy's boys. It demands self-discipline and the willingness to resist peer pressure; it requires dedication and commitment. As the surrender is given to the feminine principle, as well as to an individual woman, it goes far beyond the bedroom and the home. Gay men are as likely to submit to female authority as straight men.

It is not a new form of relationship; many men have already lived in surrender to female authority. The very fact that this text has survived shows that the people who compiled, copied, amended, printed and preserved it saw the wisdom in it. The keepers of the text did not seek to promulgate their opinions, because they were antithetical to the dominant religions, but they were so strongly motivated by the need to achieve _____ /Rectification, that they tried to live in harmony with the flow of energy through the Matrix. The material about male submission to female authority is at the heart of the text. If it had not mattered, it would have been deleted. After all, dominant groups delete from the historical record inconvenient truths, such as the power of women, unless there is profit to be made from them.

The transfer of power from men to women, as outlined in this book, needs to become a social revolution. The Matrix is an evolutionary process and humanity can collectively influence its evolution. If we shift from male domination back to female authority, we can initiate an evolutionary move away from selfishness, separation and suffering towards wholeness and unity.

This evolutionary revolution begins with women who are willing to assert authority over men, and with men who are able to empathize with, and to atone for, the distress inflicted on women, children and men over the centuries, since males usurped power.

The original writers recommended the rules outlined in Part One to govern the behaviour of a surrendered man. They may have seemed extreme when you read them for the first time, but something akin to them is necessary to ensure that men are prevented from doing any further harm to the fabric of the World of Interactions: to maximize the amount of general spiritual energy men can channel for women to use in healing the rifts and/or achieving ____ /Rectification. The rules free men from the roles for which they have proved unfit.

Better described as guidelines than rules, they are repeated again here with added comments. A lifeful woman can amend the guidelines to suit herself, but before she relaxes them, she needs be very clear that she is setting the terms and conditions of a man's surrender in accordance with her intuitive sense of what serves the unity of the whole. She must not relent because she wants to be nice, kind, lovable or loved. She has to be vigilant at all times to maintain and extend her authority.

Also, a lifeful woman needs to be aware that it is much easier for men to *say* that they want to submit, than to actually *live* in surrender. Until the words are followed by actions, they are hollow. The repetitions and rituals are included in the guidelines, because they change the neural pathways in men's brains and break the habits ingrained by centuries of male domination.

For a man who has not been raised by an authoritative woman, the first step to full surrender is to admit, verbally, how he has caused unnecessary pain to women and to the world in the past, and that he is ready to atone for his previous actions.

The woman may, at any time, test whether a man really means what he says, by asking him to do something that embarrasses him. The degree of the man's reluctance to be embarrassed is a sign of his resistance to her authority.

After accepting his surrender, the woman marks the man as hers by choosing a new name for him. She may require that he undergoes circumcision. The removal of the foreskin can only be done to a male; therefore, it is a sign of his commitment. Drastic though it is, circumcision has the advantage of helping to prevent penile cancer; tattoos are an alternative.

The second step is for the surrendered man to perform a ritual at least once a day. Women are spiritual by nature, but men need to practise. The man's daily ritual can include the acknowledgement that he is completely submissive to the woman's will, reflection on the rules that she has set for him, and if she requires it, atonement for his past behaviour in particular and the past behaviour of his gender in general. The ritual suggested by the original writers ends with these words, addressed to the woman, *"Let the actions of my body, the words of my mouth, the thoughts of my mind and the spirituality of my existence be acceptable to you now and for the rest of my life."*

One act of atonement that a woman can choose concerns finances. For as long as the current monetary system props up all patriarchal structures, a man can make amends for the financial limitations suffered by generations of women, by handing control of his money to the woman. It is an act of trust as well as a gift of valuable energy.

The third step requires the man to implement the tasks set for him by the woman. They can be active or passive, but they all serve as a constant reminder that he is under her authority and cannot deviate from her will. The very fact that he obeys her, gives a huge boost to the energy she receives from him.

The tasks govern how the surrendered man behaves towards the woman to whom he has surrendered, as well as to all women. They mean that the words with which he finishes his daily ritual have a real effect on how he conducts himself.

**The actions of the body**. The surrendered man gives control over his sexuality to the woman. Erotic fantasies about submission to a powerful female are quite common and may be what draws a man to surrender. When power really does shift from a man to a woman, sexual and domestic relationships are transformed, but male surrender cannot be based, solely or primarily, on the fulfilment of fantasies.

The surrendered man is monogamous, though the woman may choose not to be. She may accept the surrender of one man or several men. She says when, how and, indeed, if she and the man are lovers. He is sexually passive until, and unless, she asks him to be active. The text recommends that they are married, but only she can decide to end the marriage. Also, she decides which other women he may touch, and what sort of physical contact he may have with them. She may feminize him by having him wear female clothing, or in any other way she chooses.

Although expressed in a different language, this form of intimate relationship is similar to Tantra and Shaktism, which acknowledges that without Shakhti, Shiva is dead. In the full symbiotic relationship between a surrendered man and a lifeful woman, there is the recognition of the energetic flow that honours the life force – Tantra calls it the divinity – of both partners. Shakhti, the feminine, completes Shiva, the masculine.

In the west, Tantra is usually seen as a set of techniques to enhance sexual pleasure. For a surrendered man, who is in intimate relationship with a lifeful woman, his passivity means that he might not have intercourse quite as often as he wants it, but when he does, his focus on his partner's pleasure ahead of his own, brings extremes of pleasure he is unlikely to have experienced before. Simply because a woman is in charge, she is more likely to express her need for touch and non-genital pleasure, than in the past, when such a request could be interpreted as a signal for her lover to initiate intercourse. Further, his surrender means that arguments are diffused before they can start, which can free the sexual relationship from emotional tensions.

The actions of his body include how the surrendered man looks at the woman. He must not look her in the eyes without her permission. The rule exists, because eye contact is one of the means men have used to control women. Keeping his eyes downcast is an act of submission to female authority. Whether or not the man averts his eyes from the faces of all women, is up to the woman to decide.

The woman's authority over a surrendered man extends to his actions beyond the intimate and domestic spheres. His work and leisure, in fact all aspects of his life, are subject to her command. At all times, the woman needs to be vigilant to maintain and extend her authority, as male dominated patterns of gender-specific behaviour do damage and die hard. She must not permit him to add to the suffering caused by men. Even if her decisions sometimes appear arbitrary, he has to accept them without complaint. Given that it is her right and duty, as a woman, to alleviate suffering, she is unlikely to make him suffer through her choices for him.

**The words of the mouth**. How the surrendered man speaks to the woman is a crucial part of his submission to her. He will not use words to argue, persuade, complain, undermine or contradict. He will not lie or make excuses. He will accept what she says and obey her in what she asks of him. He will make comments and suggestions only when she requests them.

**The thoughts of the mind**. Thoughts are included in the ritual, because they may be as loud as spoken words. Couples in intimate relationships often know what the other is thinking, so thoughts can be very influential. A man's patterns of thought have been conditioned by centuries of male domination. As part of his on-going submission, a surrendered man needs to monitor every idea that emerges from the unconscious into consciousness. Once he notices that an idea, or a thought, comes from old, ingrained patterns of superiority and control, he needs to release it gently. Also, he needs to remember that his purpose is to serve, support and supply a lifeful woman and to atone for the wrongs he has done in the past. This is how he expresses the spirituality of his existence.

With the fourth step, the woman and the surrendered man achieve symbiosis. It happens when the man has sacrificed to the woman the one thing he possesses in the female world – himself. By this time he has learned that, when women and men disagree, the women are always right. He has discovered from experience, that female rule works so well that he does all he can to help other males to accept and adjust to it as well. At this stage, the man has overcome all his egotistical drives. He is so utterly dedicated to channelling energy to the female, that it is akin to worshipping a Goddess in the form of a living woman. She may then add the energy she receives from him to her own and use it to heal.

Paradoxically, surrender brings personal liberation from old roles for both men and women. This form of relationship takes both parties away from what harms and inhibits the flow of life through the World of Interactions towards what enhances and heals it.

Emotionally, both the man and the woman know where they stand with each other. This stability can ease the tensions that lead to rows in relationships where the partners are fighting for supremacy. When a man has found his place in the natural order, he can take great pride in the quality of his service, even when he performs repetitive domestic chores.

The purpose of this kind of relationship is more than the personal satisfaction and freedom for the individuals involved. For the original writers, the sole purpose of men's work was to free women from all responsibilities, other than their creative duties. When a man surrenders to a lifeful woman, his work is to serve, support and supply her so that she is free to do her spiritual work, which has implications far beyond the couple's domestic sphere. Backed up by the general spiritual energy that he channels to her, a lifeful woman can use her creativity to its fullest degree, to heal the rifts caused by generations of dominant males.

## FEMALE CREATIVITY

Many artists and other creative men are aware that their creativity comes from a deep connection with the feminine aspects of themselves. The muse can be a real woman, or a series of real women, or she can emerge from the "non I", but for creative men, she is the inspiration for their work. Like a lifeful woman, the muse comes and goes as she pleases and cannot be coerced. The muse may or may not be acknowledged, but no man can truly create anything without access to female energy. Without it, a man's creative works become repetitive and mechanical.

Despite the recognition of the muse's role in men's creativity, the works of creative women have been widely ignored. The original writers were of the opinion that only women create.

One of the meanings of *lifeful* is *giving vitality to*. This is part of women's spiritual work. Not only do women passively create new bodies from the substance of their own bodies, during pregnancy, they can actively *give vitality to*, or create, from the fabric of the World of Interactions.

Lifeful women are capable of generating such powerful creative energy, that they have the potential to make a very different future for the whole of humanity, especially if they collaborate with each other and have the full support of men who have surrendered.

Passive is often paired with female, while active is often paired with male, but neither pair is actually synonymous. Women can be active and, indeed, they must be to create the future they desire.

Passively and unconsciously, each of us creates the future all the time, in that we interpret what happens to us in the light of our previous experiences and beliefs. Also, we attract people and situations that reflect our worldview. For example, if we expect certain friends to be unreliable, they usually meet our expectations. Whatever each of us thinks and feels, hopes and fears, our subconscious "non I" makes every effort to deliver what it assumes we mean. The "non I" can only identify which of our emotions is the most intense, but it cannot assess the most intense emotion qualitatively. If, for instance, it decides that anger is stronger than joy, it will do its best to feed the former instead of the latter.

The original text provides the steps for lifeful women to create actively and consciously. You may have seen something similar in New Age books and online videos about manifestation or creating abundance. The New Age techniques usually offer personal fulfilment, which is a form of selfishness.

You may have experimented with these techniques and they may or may not have worked for you. If they did not work, there are several possible reasons.

* Above all, will power does not work. You may have used will power, which implies that you expected to have power *over* your future. *Power over* is the magician's manipulation, the patriarch's means of control. *Power over* and *power from within* are different. Power flows from within when you are aligned with the fabric of the World of Interactions and in the flow of the unnameable, eternal Tao. To create successfully, the power has to flow through you. You have to be connected to the whole and to feel the connection in every fibre of your being.

*Timing is crucial. As time is one name for the flow of energy through the Matrix, this is another way to emphasize that you need to be aligned with the flow in order to manifest.

*You may have underestimated the degree to which you were in fear, or in doubt, about your ability to create.

*The New Age advice tends to focus on manifesting material things like jobs, lovers, and cars. We often confuse wants with needs, not least because advertisers and sales reps have told us that we need things to make us happy and fulfilled. The desire for things may be very strong, until we realize that they are not necessary for our happiness. You will manifest what you need rather than what you want.

*You may have tried to dictate the process of how your intention was supposed to manifest. For example, if you have to travel from A to B you may focus on acquiring a car, when you actually need a means of getting from where you are to where you need to be.

*You may have been too attached to the outcome.

*The people around you may, consciously or unconsciously, not want you to create something new, because it means you will change.

The original text states that for a woman to create, she needs to be absolutely clear who she is, what she is and what she wants. In other words, you need to be free of male control, clear about your motives, and absolutely certain that you have the right and the ability to create.

The original writers outlined the process of creativity, so that women were empowered to heal and to mend rifts. They intended it to be used for the benefit of all, rather than for personal gratification. That said, a lifeful woman might use creativity in any way she sees fit, because she is in such harmony with the flow that she cannot make mistakes.

When you are lifeful — and only when — settle in a quiet meditative state to make a list of your goals. It does not matter whether your conscious mind thinks they are achievable. Write your goals down without self-censorship. There are no limits when you are truly listening to your heart.

Write only your goals. Do not drift into thinking about the stages of how they might manifest. Leave your subconscious mind free to find the most appropriate means to bring your aims into reality.

As your subconscious responds to your emotions and does all it can to meet your emotional needs, thinking about your goals is not enough. Read your list aloud, and for each item imagine its manifestation in as much detail as you can, as passionately as you can. After all, the Matrix emanated from the _____ /N-One-ness because of the strength of its desire to know itself as unity.

You may want to work with your goals in a quiet meditative state, at night and in the morning, by saying them aloud, visualizing them and desiring them.

Leave your subconscious mind to arrange how your desired goals come into your reality. Your "non I" can put all the relevant bits of information into place, so your intentions can manifest. Sometimes you will be surprised by how they happen. Your heart may prompt you to phone someone immediately. It may guide you to turn left instead of right, so that you meet someone who can help you. Your heart's suggestions may seem bizarre, but the more willingly you listen to and act on them, the more quickly your desires will manifest.

The practice can be done alone, or with a group of other women who share the same goals. Women focused together on healing and changing the world can, and will, heal and change the world without force, without coercion, without exerting power over anyone. When your intentions to create a fairer, healthier, more generous world, combine with those of other women with the same desire, the sooner it will happen. The more women who dare to establish their authority, the easier the birth of a different world will be.

Remember how emergent behaviour functions, and how significant the role of women was in the experiments on human swarming. By setting goals, you establish the vector, along which the intelligence distributed through the collective "non I" can swarm. At first, the movement may not be detectable, but somewhere along the vector the swarm gains unstoppable momentum. The changes you are creating will manifest in some form or another, although perhaps not in the form you see in your mind's eye, because at the heart of the creative process lies a paradox.

Your passion for a world rooted in the unity of all things is essential for its creation. However, it is equally important that you are not attached to the processes of its manifestation or to its achievement. It is only possible to hold the paradox – the contradictory positions of passion and detachment — when you are aligned to the flow of the Matrix. You can be both passionate about mending the world and detached from it, because you know that you, and everyone and everything in the universe, is already part of the vast consciousness.

The values on which a world created by women and led by women will be based, are those quietly fostered by women for millennia. Most likely, the values will include care for self and others, a sense of community and creativity, founded in the awareness of the oneness of all life. A more detailed description of such a world limits the possibilities.

Your head, saturated by images from the media, may try to tell you such a world is a utopian dream. It is as yet a dream, but one that women can legitimately and rightfully create.

Know in your heart that it will be so because it is time.

## THE ORIGINAL STORY

Once, or maybe more than once, before time began, the ____ /N-One-ness had the desire to know itself, and from the strength of its desire, our Matrix split from it.

Then time began its inexorable flow through all the processes required to develop individuals capable of experiencing their separation and of rediscovering the unity of consciousness.

After many trials and evolutionary errors, homo sapiens arrived in the World of Interactions about 200,000 years ago and prevailed over other types of human. The homo sapiens made clay figurines of big-breasted and big-hipped females. They scratched vulvas in cave roofs and painted cave walls with pubic triangles, as well as animals. They venerated the forces of nature and built ritual places out of massive stones.

Eventually, they gathered in settlements that grew into villages, that grew into cities. They created goddesses and gods, which reflected their deepest longings and their greatest fears.

In Sumer, the revenues collectors and the astronomers needed to keep records. They invented writing, and power passed to men who were themselves literate or could employ those who were literate.

When men began to write stories, they turned on women with hatred and blame, because women represented something that men could neither comprehend nor control. From the earliest writings, the Original Story was twisted and obscured, but it never quite disappeared.

The Original Story tells of our origins, of our purpose, of our responsibilities and of our destination. It tells us why women are powerful and why they are feared.

We, who are alive now, can see all too clearly the consequences of centuries of patriarchal control. We need to rewrite the Original Story and to retell it at every opportunity.

# PERSONAL STORIES: THE EDITOR'S TALE

In May 2011, I was reintroduced to the researcher, whom had met briefly a decade or so earlier. Revelling in the joy of meeting a like mind, we talked for hours about the overlaps and differences between the ideas contained in his translation of the original texts and my ideas and experiences.

Early in our conversations we talked about the small, but crucial, difference between aggression and assertiveness. To illustrate the difference, when I have been aggressive I have had endless, emotionally draining arguments with men. Once my nose was broken. Twice I have used rage-fuelled assertiveness with success. Once I was incandescent with fury and loud. Clearly and tersely, I ordered a very large and very angry man to leave the room before he hit a woman. He left. The other time, I was incandescent and quiet. Clearly and tersely, I explained to an obscene phone caller why he was upsetting me. He apologised.

I am telling this story, and something of my journey towards the ideas presented in this book, in the hope that it supports, validates and eases the journey of others.

My mother was a creative woman, whose creativity was sabotaged by her inner judge. She was an emotional volcano, furiously critical of everyone around her. Her example taught me to honour my need to create in images and words.

My father was an alpha male who was occasionally heard to mutter, 'Even the dog's a bitch.' The cat was female too. I was fortunate that I had no brothers. Nobody taught me to pretend I was not intelligent.

In the early 1970s, when my father was younger than I am now, we went for a walk in the hills that surrounded our home. He said that he had so much – a good job, a beautiful home, a wife and daughters he loved — but he did not know why. I resolved that by the time I reached his age I would know why.

In my teens I refused to be confirmed into the Church of England, for two reasons. The idea of eternal damnation for actions in a life that was the briefest flicker in the light of eternity seemed unjust. The second reason was more important: the Church of England had no place for the Divine Feminine.

I knew that the Goddess existed but I had to wait until I was in my early thirties  before I heard anyone else talk about her in public. Then the television Channel 4's series, *After Dark,* aired a discussion about witchcraft. Margot Adler, the Wiccan priestess and writer, was among the guests and the following week I bought one of her books. I read everything I could about feminist, Goddess-centred spirituality, though I never became a practising Wiccan.

Around that time, my father died. In our last conversation, he regretted that he had paid so little attention to the inscription at Delphi: GNOTHI SEAUTON (know thyself.) An intense experience I had the night he died, convinced me that death ends the physical body, but the soul, the spiritual essence, goes on somewhere.

The conception of my son convinced me that the spiritual essence comes from somewhere. By the time he was born, I had accepted the basic tenets of the Goddess path:

*she is the life spark in all living beings and she is much more than the ever-loving mother. She is also Kali and Sekhmet. (I have been zapped by two statues of Sekhmet in different museums and those who have had similar experiences will know exactly what I mean.)

*there is no division between spirit and matter because everything is the same energy in finer or denser form

*life cycles through birth, death and rebirth in order to become conscious of the unity of all creation

*everything, therefore everyone, is interconnected.

I had also had experiences of past lives. These experiences felt as though they came from a different part of my brain, possibly the pineal gland, compared to the source of the stories I have written. As these memories have helped me to make sense of events in my life, I am still inclined to claim them as mine, but they may equally have come to me out of the vast field of the collective unconscious. Nobody will persuade me that they are mere fiction!

Politically, rather than spiritually, I had no liking for social hierarchies, such as male above female, the rich above the poor. My first paid employment as a teenager, brought me into contact with the so-called élite and I discovered that they were as emotionally messed up as the rest of us, if not more so. No one individual is more valuable than another.

I have never had the ambition to compete in the capitalist system, because money was not the key to my happiness or fulfilment. It made more sense to me to raise my son, myself, rather than work to pay someone else to do that job. I have no regrets about working creatively at home for comparatively little income.

And then I fell into a process of internal disintegration and reconstruction. Kicking, screaming and complaining at every possible opportunity, I surrendered to the process of transformation, during which nothing I tried to do in the outer world quite worked.

Fortunately, many other people were also experiencing much the same process. Although they use different terminology, I have relied on their words to keep from going crazy. I am grateful both to my friends, especially to my close neighbour, and to the women whose blogs I read online.

I met the researcher again at the start of May 2011. In December 2011, I formally accepted his surrender. In the New Year of 2012 I began work on the adaptation of his lengthy manuscript into the short book you are reading.

The last few months seem to have stretched into a long time. My beliefs and assumptions have been stretched and extended too.

I am growing into this style of relating. It is ideal for a creative woman like me, in that there are no arguments and no guilt trips when I take the time and space I need to paint and to write. I choose when we meet and when we part. There is less tension than even in the early stages of previous relationships. There are no storms, no tears and more laughter, more joy than I have ever known.

Innately, I have always known that spirituality and sexuality are profoundly linked. I have been puzzled and saddened when men, who said they believed the same and claimed to love me, were disrespectful of my body and emotions. Before I started serious work on the book, I saw myself as the equal of a man. I never learned that I was supposed to put my partners' needs ahead of mine, and I had some tough experiences as a result. At last I am with a man who is utterly respectful because he expects and wants a female-led relationship, as well as a female-led world. Without force or coercion, I lead and he follows.

However, I was already distrustful of the male-dominated corporate world, because it is fundamentally anti-life. I did not need to be convinced that patriarchal control and all forms of power that divide in order to rule are toxic to individuals and the planet. They are unsustainable.

Artists and writers are often the first to pick up new trends that are emerging from the collective unconscious. Creative people have the responsibility to help the new to ground into this reality by giving it form.

The novels that I have written over the last 20 years are set in a country where the rulers and the ruled accept that all life is interconnected. Their society is not without contradictions and tensions, as I try to work out how the characters feel, think and act, but I do have a clear vision that such a society is sustainable and possible.

The leap from unattained equality to female superiority has felt right, yet all the same, it has taken time to let all the implications filter through my thoughts and emotions into action.

The action can be very gentle. Editing the researcher's massive amount of material into this short book and publishing it are not forceful processes, but they may be influential in creating a swarm.

The times are definitely changing. I am utterly convinced that if enough women (prior to working on this book I would have said 'enough people'), come together to create and hold the same vision of a world based on female values — connection, compassion, care, community, sustainability — we can and will have a very different world.

If we do not bother to try to create a world based on these values, we are likely to face totalitarian rule, while the degradation of the planet's natural resources continues.

Change is in the air. Change happens with astonishing suddenness.

Let's give female authority a chance.

# PERSONAL STORIES: THE RESEARCHER'S TALE

For me, the story begins during the early teens with looking at the world and asking the question 'Why are we here, why does this world exist the way it does?' The usual answer that one 'god' or other created the world was never satisfying as it led to the question why a supposedly perfect god could possibly want to create a world so imperfect. Then there was the inevitable follow-up question, that if a god created this world, then who created that god? Nor was I satisfied by the alternative answer, that it is a 'mystery' we just have to accept. I did not accept any of this but thought that the answer was out there somewhere and if I searched hard and long enough I would find it.

To begin with, I thought that if religion did not have the answers then science just might and so I became a scientist with BSc and MSc and PhDs, expecting the answers as to why we are here but I only found more questions.

So finally, I broadened my research. After 30 or so years and thousands of books, paintings, texts etc., I found my answer through the process of 'data-overlap'. This is a process by which records from different sources — different civilizations, different millennia, different locations — are compared for similar content or parts of content. Where there is an 'overlap' of content, it is noted.) The fact that only one data-overlap pile emerged, in other words, that only one story took shape, put me on the path to arcane ancient texts. It soon became clear that very few people had ever heard of them and even fewer had access to them. Intriguingly, in recent years, other publications most likely based on the source/texts that form the basis of my translation have also appeared — co-incidence?

I met the editor for the first time, briefly, about a decade ago, and was reintroduced to her about a year ago. She represented the vital missing link that existed between the male-conducted, abstract, academic translation of the texts and the need to turn this into a readable book, written by a female editor. In other words, she was needed to feminize the context of the translation. The result is this, her book.

We believe in the need for the comprehensive change of this world, the transition from male/patriarchal hierarchical power to female authority, as outlined above. So we have begun to implement the text and give it life, with the intent to present a viable example for others to follow, proof that written theory can indeed be turned into living reality.

To confirm my surrender to the editor, I signed a document, which formally transfers power from me to her.

She is in absolute control of me and, as the text states, makes decisions for both of us. The rationale is that she is fully in tune with the Matrix, on all levels, and thus is best placed to make decisions that are beneficial for both of us, and for the Matrix as a whole. In the real world that means she has full financial control and sets the framework for me to live within, while she is free to do as she pleases.

This gives her absolute control and it means that she is making all the decisions and I am doing her will. Because a woman is in tune with the Matrix energy flow, it means that my energy is channelled through her. I become feminized by her, through my servitude to her and I am liberated from tasks I cannot possibly perform. Even so, it has taken some adjusting, to surrender to her authority. The main focus in this process concerns the change in thinking and consequent verbal patterns, which, in turn, leads to the new ways of interactions and consequently implementations.

This is why the daily ritual, described in the original text, is essential. My daily ritual includes the acknowledgement that I am completely submissive to the will of the editor, the lifeful woman in my life, and reflections/meditations on the rules that she has set for me. I also reflect on how to improve in my service to the woman I regard as my Goddess. The ritual concludes with the words: *"Let the actions of my body, the words of my mouth, the thoughts of my mind and the spirituality of my existence be acceptable to You now/today and for the rest/all of my life"*.

The texts recommend certain rules to govern the behaviour of a surrendered man. As they are intended to, they give purpose and meaning to my life and *protect* me from doing any more of the damage referred to in the original text, as 'causing rifts to the fabric of the Matrix'. By following the rules I do not have to worry if I do the right or wrong thing.

The concept, that surrender brings liberation, may sound contradictory but it is not. Practical experience has proved this concept right every time, all the time, and I will never go back to the old world. For me, living under female authority is the best thing that has ever happened. There are men out there who want to surrender to women/a woman but do not know how to communicate it, mostly for fear of being misunderstood, mainly by peers, but also by women. Again, it is fear of being misunderstood that keeps them from coming forward until someone else makes the move first.

From personal experience, I am discovering that this comprehensive service to a woman, redefines what a man stands for and, as a result, I feel more of a man now, than ever before, not less, as some men might fear. Surrender has been a worldly and spiritual liberation from a peer-pressure that is headed towards a cosmic abyss. The same fear that has compelled men to try and rule this world, during the millennia – and fail time and again — is the great curse that prevents men from fully entrusting themselves to women and surrendering themselves into their authority. The importance of this surrender is that it initiates a power-shift that is *permanent*; now I have

177

experienced living with (not under) female authority I embrace it. I have found peace and a settled identity. In other words, I am becoming compatible with the general spiritual energy.

Those cases in which other men live under female authority, to one degree or another, in a cross-cultural variety of organizations worldwide, show that men did not campaign for a return to the old male structure as they found their place in Matrix at last.

In my view, a man cannot turn surrender into an excuse to be lazy and expect to get away with being passive and have women serve him. There is a marked difference between a man's surrender and a mom's boy's attempt to escape from growing up. In other words, the difference is between a man loving and serving his Goddess, versus an eternal boy seeking and needing to be loved and served by his mother indefinitely. Or, indeed, it is the difference between a male, comprehensive support for the implementation and maintenance of female authority, or an egocentric male millstone around the female neck, holding women — and men — back.

I am in comprehensive service to the woman whom I love exclusively, and thus, naturally, I place her first every time, all the time. I do so not because I am told, but because I know her link to the Matrix and the ____ /N-One-ness gives her that natural female authority.

A short time ago, while watching a programme on television about Divine Women, I suddenly experienced a, for lack of better word, vision, in which the silhouette of my Goddess, who sat to my right and slightly ahead of me, filled with, as I felt it, the essence of the ____ /N-One-ness. This was a clear demonstration that She was an individual representative of the all-powerful Matrix and that She was here and acted with the absolute authority of the Matrix and the ____ /N-One-ness. Since then, this vision has remained with me and I sincerely hope that as many men as possible may have the same experience, as it makes clear, visually and spiritually, that only comprehensive surrender and service gives men peace, identity, purpose, and meaning in this life. For me, now more than ever before, doing my Goddess's will is the only way to change from merely existing to fully being.

You will have read the section dealing with the Bitch Goddess. From long experience, I can say that neither fight nor flight, nor any attempt to wait until she calms down has any lasting effect. This is because the problems, her grievances, remain unacknowledged, unrecognized and thus unsolved. So the next outburst is just around the corner, if it ever abates that is. This leads to a very counterproductive energy field in general, and in disharmony between the man and the Goddess, in particular. The only solution is to acknowledge the Goddess's grievances by trusting in her spiritual femininity, her female authority, and surrender comprehensively to her full control concerning everything. This act of surrender will appease the Bitch in the Goddess, because it restores the natural female authority and harmonises the energy flow coming from the Matrix. Only when we men acknowledge, that only women are in full tune with this cosmic energy, because they represent the Matrix/ _____ /N-One-ness (see the vision described above), will we find a lasting, natural, peaceful and meaningful place in this world. I know that when I surrendered, the benefits for both of us become evident immediately.

For the patriarchal hierarchical system to work it needs timetables and deadlines, in other words, it depends on rigid time keeping. That this is very male becomes evident when observing women getting ready to go out (or organize an event without male input, for that matter). At the beginning, it seems to be chaotic and disorganized and men, ready to go out for the evening, often fret and despair. Yet after a seemingly drawn-out anarchic period to start with, it comes together, all of a sudden – a fact that men usually do not acknowledge, because they are so focused fretting that the whole dynamic more often than not escapes them. And that includes arriving in time for the event, just in time, but in time nevertheless. The reason is that women swarm and do not work to rigid timetables/deadlines. The dynamic works along the lines of a logarithmic curve; first nothing much seems to happen and everything seems to be disorganized/chaotic and the suddenly the pace accelerates, until the task has been achieved before most men even notice.

The female swarm way of doing things is the natural way, as this dynamic features everywhere from the development of whole civilizations (though male-run) to the way learning a new subject is achieved. Although I am aware of this fact, more often than not I fall into the swarm trap myself, and it takes a concerted effort to trust the natural female dynamic, even though it always worked out well in the end.

We, the editor and the researcher, have made the move and invite others to follow us. Our experience shows that apart from some negative reaction from the usual suspects (beta males), we had an overwhelmingly positive response.

Surrender is a progressive path from male egocentric focus to Goddess-centred focus where male service through subservience to female authority provides the spiritual harmony, which is always lacking in conventional, male-dominated relationships. The message to those males who have yet to surrender is, don't fight it! The key is to stop hesitating and to fully trust and surrender to your Goddess. Surrender brings with it a release from the bondage of the spiritually inferior male thought patterns. When the Goddess enters your male mind, you can start to reach for that true, female-based spiritual understanding. It all starts with a sincere and unshakeable willingness to surrender and serve.

Change is coming, so let it be for the better, or in the words of the editor:

Let's give female authority a chance.

## CONCLUSION

Thank you for reading this short, provocative book.

The question is,

WHAT ARE YOU GOING TO DO ABOUT IT?

Of course, you have at least three options.

*You can close the book and forget about it.

*You can argue with it. Serious and polite arguments can be sent to the editor's email address, fiona@lifefulvision.com.*You can implement its suggestions. Support is available on the website www.lifefulvision.com in the section devoted to this book.

It is indeed time for women to reclaim their innate authority and for men to relinquish their need to control. Fixed in the written word, this book outlines why the shift in roles is necessary and it suggests how the shift can happen by means of emergent behaviour.

The lifeful vision website is intended to encourage others to dare to dream a different world into being. As it can be updated regularly, it is more fluid and responsive than this book. It can reflect the shift as it emerges. After all, emergent behaviour is by its nature unpredictable.

# NOTES

1.     Ashley Montagu *The Natural Superiority Women*

2.     Alexandra Pope *www.wildgenie.com*

3.     Sobonfu E. Some *The Spirit of Intimacy*

4.     Ashley Montagu *op.cit*

5.     Marija Gimbutas, Riane Eisler et al.

6.     Piers Vitebsky *The Shaman* Duncan Baird Publishers 2001

7.     Bettany Hughes *Divine Women* BBC2 spring 2012 et al.

8.     Leonard Shlain *The Alphabet Vs The Goddess*

9.     Ilse Seibert *Women in the ancient Near East* quoted in: -

10.    Beth Troy *Legally Bound: A Study of Women's Legal Status in the Ancient Near East* (MA thesis 2004)

11.    http://sumerianshakespeare.com/1047656/105175 6.html

12.    Piers Vitebsky *The Shaman* + editor's original research + conversations with urban shamans

13.    Nelia Beth Scovill *The Liberation of Women in Religious Sources* no date www.the religiousconsultation.org

14.    Bettany Hughes *Divine Women* BBC2 spring 2012

15.     Thomas Middleton *A Mad World, My Masters* early 1600s

16.     quoted in New Statesman 3/8/11

17.     e.g. *Money as Debt* YouTube

18.     BBC R4 *Today* May 2012

19.     eg. *www.redicecreations.com*

# FURTHER READING

Jalaja Bonheim *Aphrodite's Daughters: Women's Sexual Stories and the Journey to the Soul*, Fireside 1997

Jocelyn Chaplin *Feminist Counselling In Action*, Sage Publications 1984

Michael Jessing *Inanna's Descent & Epic of Gilgamesh* (illustrated Cosmix) available from the author on Facebook or by email mixastudio@googlemail.com

Lucia Rene *www.unplugfromthe patriarchy.com*

Joanna Russ *How to Suppress Women's Writing*, The Women's Press 1984

## ACKNOWLEDGEMENTS

My thanks go first to the nameless people who had the courage to compile the original text and to preserve it for hundreds, if not thousands, of years.

I am hugely grateful to the researcher, who wishes to be anonymous. He let me loose on his translation, helped me to organize the material, and provided much needed technical support. Without him, my life would be less enjoyable and this book would not exist.

Without Zoe Meyer, IT IS TIME would not look as good as it does. Thank you Zoe and all your team at Zoesbooks.

Thanks too to the staff at the National Library of Scotland.

Finally, thanks to all the friends and family who have discussed the ideas with me and read the manuscript and who are helping me spread the word. I am so fortunate to know you and I know you do not all agree with everything I have written. You are in alphabetical order, Carolan, Carrie, Crawford, Em, Ianto, Isobel, Jenny, Kirsty, Nikki,

Susan K, Susan M, Zoe and last, out of alphabetical order, but by no means least, Will.

Nobody named above carries any responsibility for the opinions expressed in this book.